Praise for .

"A must-have in a world where technology is increasingly distancing us from others while it creates the illusion that it is doing just the opposite."
— **Anna Jedrziewski,** *Retailing Insight*

"I love this book and welcome its valuable exploration of an important topic. Loneliness is a modern-day affliction, and Kira Asatryan dives into the experience of loneliness with skill, sensitivity, and insight. The book flows beautifully through various inquiries, complemented with great questions and journal prompts at the end of each chapter. The content is honest and bold as well as compassionate. This is a refreshing and essential reading prescription for modern life."
— **Jackee Holder,** coach and creative catalyst

"Kira Asatryan's book is a lifeline for people struggling to build and maintain meaningful relationships in our plugged-in, fast-paced society. At the height of the 'app revolution' and with the proliferation of chat apps on smartphones and tablets, the ability to *really* connect with others remains critical to our personal well-being and social development. Far from being just your typical self-help book, *Stop Being Lonely* is a sociological inquiry into the nature of relationship building, providing educated advice on how to form lasting, meaningful relationships."
— **Rune Vejby,** author of *Texting in Sick: How Smartphones, Texting, and Social Media Are Changing Our Relationships*

"*Stop Being Lonely* is one of the most valuable books I've ever read, and I read a lot. It addresses a problem so common we don't even notice that it's impacting our lives. Kira Asatryan helps us see that loneliness can be destructive but that with knowledge and guidance it can be overcome. I recommend you get one copy for yourself and another for a friend or family member. Everyone needs to own a copy of this important book."
— **Jed Diamond, PhD,** author of *The Irritable Male Syndrome* and *The Enlightened Marriage*

"Kira Asatryan describes a hidden, insidious, debilitating plague of our time: loneliness. She helps us understand the cultural trends that give rise to it and the terrible toll it takes on our peace of mind. Most important, she shows the reader how to combat its damaging effects by following her simple steps to restore caring connections with loved ones. Her book is an absolute must-read for anyone wishing to deepen the quality of their relationships and their life in general."

— **Linda Bloom, LCSW,** coauthor of *101 Things I Wish I Knew When I Got Married* and *Secrets of Great Marriages*

"Despite our 24/7 connectivity to friends, families, and coworkers, many of us experience a sense of isolation and loneliness because we're not developing close relationships. Kira Asatryan's new book guides us with practical advice and simple steps to build fulfilling, deep connections in all areas of our lives."

— **Christine Hassler,** speaker, coach, and bestselling author of *Expectation Hangover*

"*Stop Being Lonely* is an accessible, soulful, and wise book about making and deepening real connections with the people in your life, including yourself. While wide-ranging in its scope, the book is also beautifully practical and specific. Its topic is of central importance in any age but especially timely as we continue to navigate our ever-changing digital world. Highly recommended."

— **Susan Raeburn, PhD,** clinical psychologist and coauthor of *Creative Recovery: A Complete Addiction Treatment Program That Uses Your Natural Creativity*

"Loneliness is a big struggle for many. In her new book, Kira Asatryan provides us a simple yet brilliant fix."

— **Dr. Charles J. Sophy,** medical director for the County of Los Angeles Department of Children and Family Services and author of *Side by Side: The Revolutionary Mother-Daughter Program for Conflict-Free Communication*

"Kira Asatryan takes you on a step-by-step journey back to where you were meant to be: to the feeling of closeness."

— **Dr. Wendy Walsh,** CNN's human behavior expert and former cohost of *The Doctors*

Stop
Being
Lonely

Stop Being Lonely

Three Simple Steps to Developing
Close Friendships and Deep Relationships

Kira Asatryan

New World Library
Novato, California

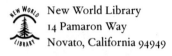

New World Library
14 Pamaron Way
Novato, California 94949

The material in this book is intended for education. No expressed or implied guarantee of the effects of the use of the recommendations can be given or liability taken. Some names have been changed to protect the privacy of individuals.

Text design by Tona Pearce Myers

Library of Congress Cataloging-in-Publication Data
Names: Asatryan, Kira, [DATE] author.
Title: Stop being lonely : three simple steps to developing close friendships and deep relationships / Kira Asatryan.
Description: Novato, California : New World Library, [2016] | Includes bibliographical references and index.
Identifiers: LCCN 2015041153 | ISBN 9781608683802 (pbk. : alk. paper) | ISBN 9781608683819 (ebook)
Subjects: LCSH: Friendship. | Interpersonal relations. | Loneliness.
Classification: LCC BF575.F66 A83 2016 | DDC 158.2—dc23
LC record available at http://lccn.loc.gov/2015041153

First printing, February 2016
ISBN 978-1-60868-380-2
Printed in Canada on 100% postconsumer-waste recycled paper

New World Library is proud to be a Gold Certified Environmentally Responsible Publisher. Publisher certification awarded by Green Press Initiative. www.greenpressinitiative.org

10   9   8   7   6   5   4   3   2

For Kaexjan, for being my kaexjan.

For Eric, for your wisdom and your typing fingers.

And for Ann, as always.

Contents

Part 4. Mastering the Art of Closeness

Introduction

A New Kind of Loneliness

For as long as humans have gathered, there have always been those who have found themselves a little on the outside. Their peers may have perceived them as different, or they may have perceived themselves as so. Relationships may have been harder for them to find, and a struggle to keep. For as long as people have attempted not to be alone, there have been those who have still been lonely.

Historically, loneliness was a result of rejection by the tribe. You had to cross some unspoken line or break a taboo to be shunned. You had to set off alarm bells in some way. There was a *reason* for one's isolation from the group and resulting loneliness, and it was a somewhat rare occurrence. Loneliness was the exception, not the rule.

Today, in the Western developed world, loneliness is becoming more the rule than the exception. Nearly everyone struggles with loneliness at some point; you'd be hard-pressed to find anyone who hasn't suffered at least a short stint of painful loneliness. You'd hardly know it, though, since loneliness no longer looks the way it once did.

Loneliness is no longer characterized by rejection from the

group or an inability to find a mate. Today, isolation is often experienced by highly functional people who have no apparent cause for feeling separate. This type of loneliness is hard to pinpoint, even by those in the throes of it. It's a new kind of loneliness, one that is not typified by a lack of people in our lives. It's an internal loneliness, a loneliness of the heart and mind.

This subtle yet troubling type of loneliness is not only elusive; it's becoming increasingly common. Most, if not all, of us have felt it at one point or another. In a moment when everything you need to do is done, you suddenly realize you have very few people with whom you can discuss the things that really matter. Maybe it dawns on you that very few people — if anyone — really know you. That very few people — if anyone — really care.

If you've struggled with this kind of loneliness, you've likely found it extremely frustrating to overcome. You want to feel less lonely, you make an effort to incorporate more people into your life, you try to connect with them, but you often walk away feeling that your efforts haven't panned out.

This new type of loneliness is not like hunger, which is always satisfied by food. Even if the meal isn't delicious, it still sates you. A stale loaf of bread satisfies true hunger as well as a freshly baked one. Yet somehow a mediocre interaction with other people does not alleviate loneliness. It usually makes it worse.

I want you to know that it's not just you feeling this way; evidence indicates that increased feelings of disconnectedness are a trend across the entire Western world. In 2006 the *American Sociological Review* reported that the average American had only 2.08 people with whom they felt they could discuss matters of importance. This number had dropped by almost a third since 1985. Researchers also found that the number of respondents who said they had *no one* to talk to about matters of importance had more than doubled, to 25 percent.

In many ways this trend is counterintuitive. Our modern world now affords us channels for communicating with anyone, anytime, anywhere. We have access to other people at unprecedented rates — rates our ancestors would have found superhuman. We no longer need to lose contact with anyone unless we want to, and if we want to, we can always meet someone new.

But the fact that we can surround ourselves with people more easily than ever before begs the question "If you and I are always available, without any practical barriers, why do I feel the barriers so intensely?"

The answer, which speaks to the heart of this new loneliness, is that the problem is not a lack of people; it's a lack of *feeling*. Specifically, the lack of one particular feeling: that of *closeness*.

When a relationship lacks closeness, you'll sense that the other person doesn't really know you and/or doesn't really care about you. Loneliness is essentially sadness caused by a lack of closeness, also known as sadness caused by distance. This is why it doesn't work to simply surround yourself with people. You must actually *feel close* to them.

The good news is that you have the power to create closeness with any willing partner, through the efforts detailed in this book. And you don't need to be a social butterfly to do this: using the techniques in this book to become just a little closer to one or two people will greatly ease your pangs of isolation.

You can create closeness with anyone who also desires it — regardless of how you met or by what title you call each other. Family member, friend, romantic partner, even coworker — anyone can become a person close to your heart, if you make the effort. You can create closeness within one of your existing relationships or within one yet to be formed.

Understanding how to do this requires a shift in perspective. We may think we have many discrete types of relationships — our relationship to a family member is different from our relationship to a business associate, for example — but when it comes to reducing loneliness, all relationships lie somewhere on the spectrum from distant to close. The closer any of these relationships are to "close," the more stable and fulfilling the relationship becomes. The more stable and fulfilling it becomes, the less lonely you feel.

As mentioned, you create closeness through specific efforts. There are actually only two actions required of you (and your partner) for becoming closer. The first is increasing your understanding of each other. The second is increasing your investment in each other's well-being. In this book, I call these two actions "knowing" and "caring."

I wrote this book to help you understand what's causing your feelings of isolation (spoiler alert: it's not your fault) and to provide you with a practical, reliable method for reducing loneliness in your life. You will learn how to start creating closeness — and in turn, to start reducing your loneliness — right now.

We'll start with the basics: understanding what closeness is and how it's generated between people, getting a sense of the benefits of having closeness in your life, and identifying obstacles to closeness in our environment. We'll then dispel some outdated myths about what alleviates loneliness and learn to identify good opportunities for creating closeness, including picking a long-term partner.

From there, we'll learn about the actions that, taken together, constitute *knowing*. These include how to:

- Have deeper conversations
- Distinguish needs and values from wants
- Ask questions that foster closeness
- Find unifying commonalities while accepting differences
- Talk productively about the past and the future
- Comfortably disclose your inner world

We'll then move on to the acts that, taken together, constitute *caring*. These include learning to:

- Feel and identify emotions
- Experience empathy
- Bond deeply with another without losing your identity
- Show someone explicitly that you care
- Handle disagreements while still communicating caring
- Maintain the bond of caring over a long period of time

You'll then learn how the principles of knowing and caring apply in different situations: at work, in romantic relationships, and with your friends and family. Last, you'll learn how to create closeness in the most important relationship of all: the one with yourself.

The loneliness that you and many others are experiencing is a new phenomenon and therefore requires a new solution. Closeness is that solution. The method laid out here will show you how to create closeness with anyone you choose, as long as the one you choose wants to create it with you too. You really can have fulfilling, long-lasting relationships. Let's learn how!

Part 1

Understanding
Closeness

Chapter 1

What Is Closeness?

Closeness is a fundamental yet little understood aspect of relationship health. It is instrumental in making a relationship feel satisfying and secure. In fact, it wouldn't be wrong to say that closeness is *the* foundation of all stable and functional relationships — romantic, familial, platonic, and business.

Yet one of the beliefs our society holds most dear is that relationships are complicated. Not just romantic relationships, either — *all* relationships are fraught with intractable complexities. Watch any movie, read any novel, and you'll begin to believe that even the best relationships are balancing on the edge. Your boyfriend becomes your husband, and suddenly you feel trapped. Your coworker becomes your boss, and now your relationship feels different. One wrong move, and your best friend could become your worst enemy.

We accept this notion implicitly, but isn't it a bit odd, when you think about it? Why would we believe that all relationships, even the ones we perceive as most solid, are teetering on the brink of calamity? Are relationships really this confusing?

"I love him. He just doesn't get me at all."

"I definitely want to marry her. I'm just worried we don't care about the same things."

"My mom is my best friend. She just can't really say anything nice."

People from all walks of life struggle with this cognitive dissonance. Can I love my girlfriend but deeply disagree with her choices? Can family really be most important if mine doesn't accept me? Can I care about my business partner but not fully trust him? These questions all point toward the same, bigger question: Can relationships ever be easy and simple? Yes, they can...when they are rooted in a foundation of closeness.

Closeness is a simple principle: it is the experience of having direct access to another person's inner world. When you have this access to another's inner world — and she has access to yours — you share the feeling of closeness.

A person's inner world includes her thoughts, feelings, beliefs, preferences, rhythms, fantasies, narratives, and experiences. When two people are close, he knows her beliefs and can easily speak to them. She recognizes his rhythms and can easily move in time with him. He can feel her feelings. She knows what he's thinking. Your inner worlds are — metaphorically — close enough to touch.

The more you gain access to someone's inner world (and she to yours), the closer the relationship with that person becomes. The more closeness you generate, the farther you move away from feeling distant. And since loneliness is essentially sadness caused by distance, the more access you gain to another person's inner world, the less lonely you will feel. In other words, closeness works as the antidote to loneliness by nullifying distance and the sadness that comes with it.

Knowing and Caring

Though it may sound like it, closeness is not magic. The process of gaining access to another person's inner world takes place because of specific efforts: the work of knowing each other and caring about each other.

Here I'd like to note that I'm using *knowing* and *caring* in their verb forms (as opposed to the static "I know you" and "I care about you"). Knowing and caring must be *done*, over and over again. You can't get to know someone well at one moment in his life and expect to still feel close to him ten years later. A long-term close relationship requires regular participation in the acts of knowing and caring.

Knowing — the kind that generates closeness — is the act of understanding another person from that person's own perspective. It's the ability to recount another person's experience of the world in his own words. Knowing someone well creates the cognitive component of closeness. It is the thing that, over time, allows you to sit next to your business partner and know exactly what she's thinking.

This way of knowing is substantially different from how we usually "know" people. We tend to think we know someone when we've interacted with him a lot and formulated a theory about "how he is." Howard is a pushover. Ashley is always late. Jenny can't control her temper. Luke is a really nice guy.

This kind of false knowing will not generate closeness. It's false because an objective, omniscient picture of "how Jenny is" doesn't exist (or if it does exist, it's unknowable to any of us). We only have our *experience* of how Jenny is. When you tell the tale of how another person is from your perspective, you're making him or her into a character, a player in your own life story. This way of knowing does not bring you closer because it is really all about you.

Let's consider Ashley, our friend who's always late. You can think you know how she is because you know she's late a lot. But you don't *really* know Ashley until you can describe her experience of her lateness from her perspective. From her perspective, she often ends up running late because she tries to do too much. She thinks she can get that second load of laundry done or write that tenth email before heading out the door. Your version of the story is "Ashley is always late." Her version is "I always try to do too much."

Knowing in this way is a powerful tool for creating closeness, because once you're able to see your friend's experience from her perspective, she can trust that if she lets you into parts of her inner world — her beliefs, narratives, preferences — you won't misinterpret them. The feeling of being misunderstood or misrepresented ("Ashley is always late. Howard is a pushover.") is one of the main factors that drive people apart. Feeling truly known, however, brings people together.

Feeling truly cared about also brings people together and mitigates loneliness. Caring — the kind that creates closeness — means being able to feel and *show* that the other person's well-being matters to you. Well-being encompasses the whole person, from his health and safety to his fulfillment and happiness. Caring about the whole person creates the emotional component of closeness. It is what allows you to look into your sister's eyes and feel what she's feeling.

The first aspect of caring — feeling the *feeling* of caring — starts with empathy. For many of us, this comes quite naturally. It can be very hard to watch someone you know well go through a struggle and not feel some empathy. If empathizing comes easily for you, it's a skill that will greatly benefit you in your pursuit of closeness. If it doesn't, don't worry — this book will provide you with strategies for improving your emotional receptiveness.

Feeling the feeling of caring extends beyond simple empathy, though. It also means feeling the *importance* of another person's health and happiness. It means you feel the gravity — the *weight* — of caring about his well-being. Feeling this sense of importance will ultimately move you into the second phase of caring: showing the other person you care.

Many of the ways we attempt this second phase — showing someone we care — are fraught with problems. It is in this phase where caring frequently falls apart in relationships because we've all learned lessons about how to show concern that are ineffective in creating closeness. In your own life, you've likely found that moments when you feel truly cared about are few and far between. Let's talk about why.

Many of us have been taught to show caring by worrying about the other person, which doesn't truly create closeness because it prompts her to prove that everything is okay with her to ease your discomfort. In addition, we may try to show caring through advising or attempting to fix the other person's problems, which doesn't work for creating closeness because it places you in a superior position, *the one who can fix things*, seeding resentment in the other person.

Real closeness requires you to adopt a new perspective on showing care in which you actively pay attention to another person's well-being and then tell her what you see. You pay attention to how he's doing, then let him know what you've noticed. It is not sharing your worries about what you've noticed. It is not trying to fix what you've noticed. It's just expressed, thoughtful noticing.

Showing care really is that simple. And luckily, because it is that simple, we can do it in many more contexts than we normally find appropriate for showing care. We can easily show our care in this new way at work, for example. Let's say you notice that one of your coworkers, who's usually gregarious, is unusually quiet one day. Showing care would entail stopping by her desk and sharing your observation: "Nancy, I noticed you're extra quiet today. You doing okay?"

A simple, interested observation, coupled with an invitation to share, is appropriate in any context. Though caring is an emotional experience, to be sure, it doesn't have to be "intimate" in the way we usually understand the word. It's just noticing and communicating interest in how another person is doing. You can absolutely be professional and still care.

Caring in this way is a powerful tool for creating closeness because it demonstrates a desire not only to know about someone's deepest inner self but also to value it. You show your spouse, friend, sister, or colleague that you care enough to notice what's going on in his or her life. Caring is, in many ways, the ultimate form of validation. Coupled with knowing, it produces an unshakable bond.

Knowing and caring can each be practiced on their own, but both are required to create true closeness. Without knowing, you may believe that a certain person cares about you but that he doesn't really "get" you — a type of caring that is easily dismissed. Without caring, you may feel mentally connected to another but feel emotionally neglected. In other words, you may feel understood, but you won't feel like you matter.

Caring without knowing often presents itself as annoyance and dismissiveness: "I know my dad loves me, but he doesn't actually understand anything about my life." Knowing without caring often shows itself as sadness and hurt: "How can my best friend — who knows literally everything about me — not realize that I'm suffering?"

Knowing and caring are a powerful combination. They create the feeling that another person not only knows your deepest, truest self, but is actively engaged in keeping your deepest, truest self well. What more could we want from our relationships?

The Benefits of Closeness

It's hard to overstate the benefits of relationships that include knowing and caring. Beyond reducing loneliness in our social lives, closeness, as we intuitively know, is vital to leading a happy life. Those of us who are creative surely remember writing a poem, drawing a picture, or singing a song about longing for closeness, as well as love, intimacy, and connection. Art has no more fruitful topics than these.

In many ways, art is all about expressing the joy of close relationships — and the sorrow of losing them — but science has something to say about the benefits of closeness as well. My favorite explanation of these benefits was offered by psychologist John Bowlby, known for his pioneering work in attachment theory. He summarizes the importance of close relationships like this: "True intimacy with others is one of the highest values of human existence; there may be nothing more important for the well-being and optimal functioning of human beings than intimate relationships."

"Well-being" and "optimal functioning" are not fanciful notions. They're not abstract constructs of the imagination or ambitions that are too lofty for us to achieve. They are simply the things that make us feel well and do well in life. They are *practical benefits*. They are the difference between being excited to get up each day and being unable to drag yourself out of bed. They are the difference between feeling happy and feeling sad, between feeling capable and feeling incapable. And they are closely related to intimate relationships.

The vast library of scientific research on relationships has demonstrated that there are at last three measurable, practical benefits to having strong ties to other people: better mental health, better physical health, and longer life. These benefits, coupled with the deep personal satisfaction that comes with feeling truly known and truly cared about, makes closeness essential for a long, happy life.

The connection between closeness and better mental health was established through one of the longest-running and best-funded social science research projects of our age: the Harvard Grant Study. The study was launched in 1938 to "discover what factors lead to an 'optimum' life." It was led by psychiatrist George Vaillant and a team of medical researchers, who followed 268 Harvard sophomores from the all-male classes of 1939–1944. The team tracked every aspect of these men's lives for the next seventy-five years.

The participants in the Grant Study were chosen because they "were healthy in body and mind, and deemed likely to capitalize on their potential and become successful adults." But not all of them sustained, or even began, happy lives. Many succumbed to alcoholism. Some remained overburdened by traumatic childhood experiences. But the ones who did succeed, both professionally and personally, all had one thing in common: highly valued close relationships. As Vaillant put it: "It was the capacity for intimate relationships that predicted flourishing in all aspects of these men's lives."

If we categorize "happiness in life" as a significant component of mental health, it becomes clear that intimate relationships contribute greatly to mental health. Closeness eases the anxiety and depression of believing that no one really cares about you. It softens the frustration and anger that come with feeling that no one understands you. Suddenly, others become available to us. Suddenly, we feel better inside.

In addition to promoting mental health, there are proven physical and biological advantages to reducing loneliness. Loneliness has been found to tax the immune system, in much the same way chronic stress does, making it less able to ward off infections. Lisa Jaremka, the lead researcher of a study on this topic conducted at the Institute for Behavioral Medicine Research at Ohio State University, reported: "We saw consistency in the sense that more lonely people in both studies had more inflammation than less lonely people. It's also important to remember the flip side, which is that people who feel very socially connected are experiencing more positive outcomes."

It's not terribly surprising that loneliness acts in the body in much the same way that stress does. In many ways loneliness *is* stressful. When you find yourself wondering, "Who could I call if I really needed someone?" it *is* stressful. For this reason, increasing the amount of closeness in your life will have much the same effect as *relaxing* when you're stressed. It will come as a relief to believe that others are truly available to you.

This increase in overall happiness and reduction of harmful stress among people with close relationships leads them to live longer. In 2010 psychology professors Julianne Holt-Lunstad and Timothy B. Smith found that the quality of one's relationships is a primary factor in longevity: "[Our] findings indicate that the influence of social relationships on the risk of death are comparable with well-established risk factors for mortality such as smoking and alcohol consumption and exceed the influence of other risk factors such as physical inactivity and obesity."

You have likely done a good job of living well and having successes, despite bouts of loneliness. You've likely learned to shelve feelings of being misunderstood or neglected by others. But your life would be substantially better — mentally and physically — if you didn't have to. Luckily, with the skills you will learn in this book, you *don't* have to.

Questions for Reflection

- Think of a time when you believed another person really "got" you. How did you feel toward her? How did she make you feel about yourself?
- Whom would you say you care about most in this world? Do you believe he knows that you care?
- In what ways has feeling distant from others affected your life?

 ## An Exercise to Challenge Yourself

Get organized about how the people in your life measure up in terms of closeness. Jot down four lists:

1. Those whom you know well
2. Those whom you feel *know you* well
3. Those whom you care about
4. Those whom you feel *care about you*

Keep these lists handy for later when we discuss picking closeness partners.

Chapter Summary

- Closeness is the experience of having direct access to another person's inner world. It is the foundation of *all* stable and functional relationships — romantic, familial, platonic, and business. Since loneliness is essentially

sadness caused by distance, closeness works as the antidote to loneliness by nullifying distance and the sadness
that comes with it.

- Knowing and caring are the two activities that generate closeness. Knowing is the act of understanding another person from that person's own perspective. Caring
means being able to feel *and show* that the other person's
well-being matters to you. Taken together, these two actions demonstrate a desire to know someone else's deepest self and to keep that self well.

- There are at least three measurable, practical benefits
to having strong ties to other people: improved mental
health, improved physical health, and longer life. These
practical benefits, coupled with the deep satisfaction that
comes with feeling truly known and truly cared about,
make closeness essential for a long, happy life.

Chapter 2

An Environment of Obstacles

Before we dive into the specifics of how to cultivate closeness, we need to understand what's causing this new type of loneliness. Understanding the problem helps us to invent better solutions.

We are not experiencing this new type of loneliness because we are somehow worse people than our ancestors were. We are not intrinsically more distant from one another; we are not inherently more reserved. In fact, we probably yearn for closeness *more* than past generations did.

We are experiencing this loneliness — more and more every year — because our social environment is changing rapidly in ways that hinder the natural generation of closeness. Our social world is very different from what it was in the past. Most young people leave their hometowns for better opportunities, living with family past a certain age is considered a failure, and big commitments such as marriage and having children are being delayed longer than they ever have before. These interruptions in our childhood relationships, coupled with a delay in forming adult relationships, profoundly affect how much closeness we feel is available to us.

While these social changes certainly matter, the single biggest environmental change to affect our levels of loneliness is the proliferation of personal technology. I believe this is the biggest factor — by far. Technology has never been so much a part of our lives as it is now. It has never been so integrated into our routines, our reasoning, and our relationships. The products of personal technology — specifically the Internet, mobile phones, and social networks — are always in our homes and in our hands. They are always on our minds.

Personal technology has undoubtedly provided us with advances too numerous to list here. You can probably think of a dozen ways your phone and the internet have made your life better. But I propose that personal technology has also built obstacles into our social lives that prevent the natural generation of closeness between people. The bad news is that this means you will need to make a conscious effort to overcome these obstacles. The good news is that your loneliness is really, truly not your fault.

You are not lonely because you are less likable than your grandparents were. You are not lonely because you are flawed. You are lonely primarily because your environment is working against you.

There are three specific ways in which technology is making it harder for us to get — and stay — close:

1. Mediated interaction (interaction through a device) is becoming the norm.
2. Technology is teaching us certain lessons that are not helpful for creating closeness.
3. Technology is reducing our natural opportunities to get close.

Let's talk a little about each one.

Obstacle 1: Mediated Interaction

More and more, our default mode of interacting with one another is through a mediator — a device. This is the first way in which personal technology is putting up roadblocks to closeness: it is making mediated interaction the norm. Mediated interaction, by definition, is not direct access to one another. Remember, closeness is defined as direct access to another person's inner world. The more we replace in-person closeness with mediated interaction, the harder it is to understand anyone else's inner world — or for them to understand yours.

If mediated interaction were simply making a phone call or video chatting while saving up for a plane ticket to visit friends and family, I wouldn't see it as exacerbating loneliness. Technology is extremely useful for keeping relationships going in between periods of in-person togetherness. The issue is that mediated interaction is *replacing* in-person togetherness. Phone calls and video chats become a problem when they start replacing plane tickets all together.

One type of mediated interaction that deserves special attention here is social networks — Facebook, Twitter, Pinterest, Instagram, to name just a few. In some ways the combination of mobile phones and social networks is the perfect storm of mediated interaction. It feels *so* much like you have people around. You can feel as if you are carrying people around in your pocket at all times. But is this ability really making you happy? Is it really making you feel less alone?

Tell me you haven't felt disappointed when someone close to you posts on your Facebook wall instead of calling to wish you a happy birthday. Tell me you haven't found it annoying when someone repeatedly "likes" your Instagram posts while simultaneously ignoring your attempts to hang out. Maybe you've gotten excited about someone you met on a social network, only to find out it was all smoke and mirrors. We've all received an email or text from a friend with an odd tension to it. It's too short or too brusque, or just…off. A slightly accusatory tone? Maybe she's mad at me. She's mad. I'm pretty sure she is.

These are the barriers — the mental and emotional ones — we sense even after all practical barriers have been removed. It feels as if there are barriers because of our core point here: we do not really have direct access to one another.

We cannot feel what another person is feeling over Instagram. We cannot understand what our friend is thinking over Pinterest. We cannot embrace each other over Skype. You cannot really know and care through a screen.

Misinterpretations and misunderstandings are a more innocent result of technology's lack of direct access. A more nefarious result is intentional secrecy. It's been proven that everyone lies on online dating profiles, but generally just a little bit — an inch of height here and a few pounds there — nothing important. And it's not as if people can't lie in person; they certainly can. But they can't lie nearly as much in person as they can online.

The secrecy afforded by technology has become something of a novelty. We've never been allowed to be this anonymous with one another before, and we're starting to see anonymity as a fun pastime.

Just nine months after its launch, a mobile app called Secret raised $35 million in funding. Secret is exactly what it sounds like. It allows you to tell your friends (and friends-of-friends and neighbors) your secrets, while remaining anonymous. The company that created a similar app — Whisper — was named one of "the World's Most Innovative Companies in Social Media" by *Fast Company* in 2014. Secret's tagline says it all: "Share anonymously with friends, co-workers and people nearby. Find out what your friends are really thinking and feeling."

Find out what your friends are really thinking and feeling. It's a mind-boggling statement, when you think about it. It implies that somehow, despite our unprecedented levels of access to one another, we actually know *less* about what we are all *really* thinking and feeling.

These anonymous apps are not the only social media that make our interactions flimsier. The king of the fleeting interaction and fastest-growing app of 2014 — Snapchat — allows messages to be viewed for only ten seconds or less. Sobrr, one of the fastest-growing seed companies of 2014, enables "users to create ephemeral online friendships through messaging and photo sharing. These 24-hour friendships expire unless both parties agree to continue."

Are these apps fun and entertaining? Yes. Are they popular? Definitely. Do they function in a way that's inherently dysfunctional for communicating about anything that matters? I'd say so. Are they helping us build satisfying relationships? Not really.

Mediated interaction can be treacherous. In essence, it gives you the sensation of having more people around you than are physically present. Social networks can convince you that you have people in your life. This makes it all the more disturbing if you then wake up one day and find yourself profoundly lonely.

Luckily, the way to overcome the obstacle of mediated interaction is relatively simple: we need to view mediated interaction as something we use *in service of* in-person interaction. Technology should not be shunned — quite the opposite! Used in the right way, connecting via technology can help you have more closeness in your life. It just depends on how you use it.

The first step in using technological connectedness in service of closeness is adding layers of communication back in. Even when we're doing our best to be honest and straightforward, connecting through an intermediary — a chat client, for example — removes layers of communication that people need in order to get to know one another well.

The value of voice tone, body language, facial expression, and emotional signals should not be underestimated. By some accounts, nonexplicit communication makes up 93 percent of the messages we receive. If you have a choice between simple words and words plus voice tone, go with the more layered choice. If you can add facial expression in, go for it. The more layers the better.

I also recommend reserving technological connectedness for maintaining an already close relationship, as opposed to using technology to create one. It's extremely difficult to do the work of knowing and caring if you and the other person are not in the same physical space. But devices do remove many of the limitations of distance, travel, time zones, and overall busy lives. If used in the right way, they can help keep your hearts and minds close while your physical selves are distant.

Obstacle 2:
The Lessons Technology Is Teaching Us

The second way in which technology is getting in the way of closeness is that it's changing the way we think. Many of us — particularly those of us in the Millennial generation — feel that computers and mobile phones have helped to educate us about the world. While we may believe our computers and phones are just gadgets — nothing more than glorified toys — this really is not the case. Computers are not just gadgets. Computers are our teachers.

The more we interact with our personal technology, the more we develop what I call a "technology mind-set." This mind-set does not stop influencing us when we put down our phones. When we are constantly learning lessons about how to interact using our devices, those lessons spill over into our face-to-face interactions with people. Unfortunately, many of the lessons we're learning are not helpful for creating closeness with real people in real life.

The primary lesson we are learning from technology — one that is particularly unhelpful in creating closeness — is the principle of efficiency. Google defines the word *efficient* as "achieving maximum productivity with minimum wasted effort or expense." This principle is core to making a good personal technology product. Think of how efficient interacting with your iPhone can be. You have to do exceptionally little to get what you want out of your phone. When we're required to perform an extra step to find the thing we're looking for, the annoyance we often feel is palpable.

Efficiency is a wonderful principle for making great tech products. The issue is that nothing lives in isolation. As we integrate these products deeper into our lives, the central principle they were built around — efficiency — seeps deeper and deeper into our minds. The more we expect perfect efficiency from interactions with our phones, the less patience we have for interactions with people.

My hometown in Silicon Valley has embraced the values of technology more completely than anywhere else, but we are not alone. People may not realize it, but the values of their iPhones have influenced their own values — and by extension the way they think about relationships. Interaction should be useful. It should get you closer to something you want — something beyond the interaction itself. And if you think it'll be a waste of time or energy, you shouldn't bother.

These values have prompted many of us to be much more wary of "unnecessary" human interaction. People might slow you down or just add a layer of annoyance to your day — like an extra step to open your camera on your phone. In the business of making successful devices, this is probably the right way to think. But what is this mind-set doing to our relationships? What is it doing to our hearts?

If removing unnecessary interactions left us with more time and energy to pursue meaningful interactions, this way of thinking would not pose much of a challenge to relationships. It could even improve them! Weeding out the most superficial interactions could leave more energy for deeper, closer ones.

But if that were the reality, we'd see an increase in the number of deeper relationships being reported...and we don't. A comprehensive study published by *AARP The Magazine* in 2010 found that 35 percent of adults over the age of forty-five were chronically lonely, as opposed to only 20 percent in the 1980s.

And the numbers are even more dramatic for Millennials — those born between 1981 and 1997 — since they are the generation most entrenched in personal technology. Also in 2010 the Mental Health Foundation published a "Lonely Society" report, which found that "nearly 60% of those aged 18 to 34 questioned spoke of feeling lonely often or sometimes, compared to 35% of those aged over 55." The report called the generational differences "striking."

The reality is, the types of human interactions that generate closeness and reduce loneliness are not terribly efficient...and measuring the success of a human interaction by that benchmark helps to keep us lonely. We will need to unlearn some of the lessons technology has taught us in recent decades and relearn how to get close to one another.

Obstacle 3: Reduction of Our Natural Opportunities to Get Close

Beyond changing the way we think, technology is propagating yet another obstacle to closeness: it has unwittingly reduced our opportunities for getting close through natural circumstances. We really don't *need* to interact with people much anymore. When it comes to getting essentials done — eating, shopping for goods, cleaning our clothes, getting around town — we can handle almost every task on our own.

In past generations, friendships and other kinds of relationships would arise organically when we ran into one another in our communities. But today we no longer need to *be in* our physical communities. We don't need to go to a restaurant, since we can have our food delivered. We don't need to go to a classroom to take a class, since we can take the class online. We don't need to shop in stores, since we can order everything from Amazon. We don't even need to go to a workplace to work.

As someone who's lived and worked in Silicon Valley my whole life, I've seen the effect of this trend firsthand. In the modern workplace — the one championed by Silicon Valley — remote working is customary. Even the smallest start-ups have at least some employees working remotely at all times. As the tools and technology for remote working improve, teams can certainly complete their projects despite physical separation. The work will get done. But how is the slow dissolution of our work communities affecting us? How does it feel to work with people you can't really get to know?

When I ponder these questions, I think of the time Marissa Mayer, CEO of Yahoo, ordered all employees who worked remotely to get back into the office or face termination. The move was criticized as a step backward for the modern workplace.

How could a technology company reject the very advances it had helped to create?

Yet if you spoke to anyone who worked at Yahoo! at the time (as I did), you'd hear nothing but praise for the decision. As my friend who worked on Yahoo!'s mobile team put it, "The remote workers really were like nonentities. I would email these people every day and have calls with them every week, but if they'd passed me on the street I'd never have known it was them. It's hard to make a company culture with ghosts."

Of course, there are undeniable benefits to working from home, especially for parents. Most employers recognize these benefits and have encouraged more and more of their employees to work remotely. But while the benefits of remote working are undeniable, it's also hard to deny that it's substantially harder to get to know or start to care about coworkers when you never see them. I don't imagine any former on-site employee would say he felt closer to his coworkers after he moved off-site.

And maybe you don't even want to; after all, it's not required to have a warm, close relationship with your colleagues. But what if you did? Wouldn't it feel wonderful to know you had at least a few people available between 9:00 and 5:00, Monday through Friday, to talk to about something that matters? If you were not close to any of your coworkers, wouldn't that be a missed opportunity?

Work may be just one missed opportunity for close relationships — one that we could theoretically make up for in other areas of our lives. If working from home increased closeness within our family, there would be little effect on our overall loneliness levels. The problem is that technology is erasing many of our opportunities to get close — so many that we hardly know where to find *any* organic opportunities at all.

For these missed opportunities, seen as small sacrifices for the larger benefit of a more efficient life, really do add up. It *is* harder to make friends when you don't get coffee with your coworkers before your morning meeting. It *is* harder to have a magical moment with a stranger when you never meet any strangers. You *will* be lonelier if you never see anyone face-to-face.

This lack of organic opportunities for closeness is a huge part of why you're struggling with loneliness. The good news is that you have it within you to create new opportunities. The people who will someday know you well and care about you deeply are already out there. Let's learn how to find them!

Questions for Reflection

- When you're feeling lonely, what do you do to comfort yourself? Do any of these strategies involve your computer or your phone?
- Which relationship in your life — new or old — needs to be taken off-line?
- In what area of your life could you start creating opportunities for more closeness?

 ## An Exercise to Challenge Yourself

Pick a way to limit your device time that still works with your lifestyle. Some ideas include "device bedtime" — turning your devices off after 9:00 each evening; "device Sabbath" — turning your devices off on Saturdays or Sundays (or any other day that feels right to you); and "device sabbatical" — taking a full week off from technology once or twice a year.

Chapter Summary

We are not lonely because we are flawed; our tech-centric environment is working against us in three specific ways:

1. **It promotes mediated access, not direct access.** More and more, interacting with other people through a device is becoming the norm and is replacing in-person interaction. This poses a problem because it's extremely difficult, if not impossible, to access each other's inner worlds through a device.

2. **It is teaching us new and unhelpful lessons about how to interact.** Tech products value efficiency above all else. Because we interact with tech products so much now, we are learning to believe all interactions should be efficient above all else — a technology mind-set that does not lend itself well to creating closeness.

3. **It is reducing our natural opportunities to get close.** Technology has made it so that we no longer *need* people the way we once did. We no longer need to be in our physical communities the way we once did. This reduces spontaneous opportunities to get close to others.

Chapter 3

Dispelling Old Myths

Now you understand the basic framework for reducing loneliness: closeness is what you've been craving, you can attain it through increased mutual knowing and caring of others, and your technological environment is getting in your way. Before we move on to the practicalities of creating the closeness we all crave — starting with how to pick partners — we need to let go of some outdated ideas about what "should" alleviate loneliness. These myths will trip you up along the way if you don't first work to dispel them.

Most of us grow up believing in certain "solutions to loneliness" that we know from experience fail as often as they succeed. And when they fail, we blame either ourselves or the other people involved... when in reality, we should be pointing a finger at the solutions themselves.

This is a new kind of loneliness that requires a new solution. In this chapter we will work to dismantle the top three outdated myths about what we should be doing — and to whom we should be looking — to feel less lonely.

1. **Love is a reliable solution to loneliness.** You may be wondering why I maintain that the antidote to loneliness is closeness and not love. Yes, love is a powerful, ecstatic force that brings people together. Love is one of the highest highs human beings can experience. But can you be in love with someone and still feel lonely in your beloved's presence? Absolutely.

2. **Some types of relationships are inherently closer than others.** Most of us believe that some relationships should feel close — particularly family relationships. But is believing this a reliable solution to the problem of loneliness? Someone can have two living parents, three siblings, and a spouse — and still feel desperately alone.

3. **If you're lonely, just be around people.** It sounds so simple. Just put yourself out there! Can it feel refreshing to work from a coffee shop instead of at home, alone? Of course. Does it feel great to work on a team of smart people? Yes...usually. Does a rapid hiring spree at work make you feel less isolated? Not really. Could any of these situations actually make you feel lonelier than you feel just being alone? They definitely could.

All these myths contain a grain of truth and a mountain of misinterpretations. I'll show you how to unlearn the useless parts and grab hold of the stuff that works. Let's get started.

Myth 1:
Love Is a Reliable Solution to Loneliness

You may have been wondering why I have yet to mention love in our discussion of loneliness. Isn't love a perfectly good solution to loneliness? Isn't love the deepest, strongest bond we can have with another person? Isn't love the basis of all relationships that matter?

The answer is the same to all these questions: yes and no. Love absolutely brings people together. When someone who's been a stranger becomes a lover, in our eyes he becomes infused with an almost surreal importance. It can be hard to tell where you end and he begins...and you both like it that way.

But the majestic, heightened state of love has a flip side, one with which we're all too familiar. Love is fickle. You could fall in love with someone who's completely inappropriate for you. You could fall in love with someone who's not available. You could love someone who doesn't love you back. You could love someone passionately for a short period of time and then watch the relationship fizzle for reasons you don't fully understand.

And it's not just romantic love that's largely outside of our understanding. Expectant parents will attest to the fact that we can love someone before he's even born. We can love people after they die. Whom we love (and for that matter, when, where, how, and why we love) is largely outside our control. The notion that love is a reliable solution to loneliness is a myth because, simply put: love is a mystery. Closeness, however, is not.

We can pick up methods for creating closeness because we know what generates closeness between people and what doesn't. I don't think anyone can say the same about love. Love certainly reduces loneliness, given the right circumstances, but it also increases loneliness under unfavorable ones. Closeness, unlike love, always works toward reducing loneliness. Closeness is *useful* in a way that love is not. If you do certain tangible things with a receptive partner, you will see tangible results. The more effort you put into it, the more you will get out of it.

There's also a specific way in which closeness is a handier solution than love: it opens up the possibility of less loneliness at work. It's generally deemed inappropriate to love anyone at work. Even if you do have a strong connection or friendship with a colleague, it's easy to see how calling it "love" makes the relationship instantly sound unprofessional.

But most of us spend a great deal of time at work, and there are likely lots of people we know professionally with whom we could build a meaningful relationship. Closeness gives working relationships the opportunity to matter as much as strictly personal ones.

The fact is, you don't have to be lonely just because you're not in love. And if you are in love, closeness makes that love that much more stable and reliable.

I see evidence for this point in the ample research that's been done on marriage and divorce. The overwhelming majority of people who get married, at least in Western developed countries, say that they are doing it for love. In our culture marriage is seen as the ultimate expression of committed love. Most who commit to marriage also expect that the love that brought them together will last a lifetime.

Let's pair this fact about how marriages begin with what we know about how they end. The Divorce Mediation survey conducted by Lynn Gigy and Joan Kelly found that 80 percent of divorced people said their marriages broke up *primarily* because they "grew apart." This cause trumped all others, including the one we generally think of as the main marriage killer: affairs. Only 25 percent of respondents said an affair played any part in the decline of the marriage.

So what does this tell us? Marriage is all about love and divorce is all about *distance*. Even the relationships that are most filled with love will fall apart without closeness. Closeness is the foundation for all satisfying and long-lasting relationships because love really *needs* closeness in a way that closeness doesn't need love.

You *can* feel close to someone you're not in love with. And if you're in love but can't access your partner's inner world, it's inevitable that the relationship will slide down the spectrum to distance.

That being said, love relationships — particularly marriages — *are* excellent opportunities to create closeness. The great advantage marriage has over other relationships is that it's an explicit commitment. It's one of the few times (maybe the only time?) when you expressly choose a partner and they choose you back. This creates an environment of deliberateness — of conscious choosing — that is very conducive to creating closeness.

But don't wait for a love relationship to find you before you can stop feeling lonely. You can create so much fulfillment and connection with others without waiting for love.

Myth 1: Love is a reliable solution to loneliness.
Myth 1 reframed: Love is a mystery; closeness is not.

Myth 2: Some Types of Relationships Are Inherently Closer Than Others

If there's one type of relationship we think *should* feel closer than others, it's our relationship with family members. And there are perfectly good reasons why we assume this. Family relationships are the first relationships we experience, and, unlike coworkers, Twitter followers, or significant others, family has the advantage of having mattered for millions of years.

The earliest evidence of family life — specifically figurines of mothers and children — dates back to the thirteenth millennium BCE, making them as old as civilization itself. For all intents and purposes, family has always existed. Moreover, it's always been a necessary social unit. In another time and place, a person would die without a family. If one were hungry or needed shelter, he'd go to his family. If someone wanted to marry or fell ill, she'd look to her family. It only makes sense that if someone were lonely, he'd find relief with his family, right?

If you happen to have close relationships with most of your family members, you probably think so. Parents are basically required to be there for you, right? Siblings can be really fun to vent with. Sure, you might have a close-minded grandparent who isn't terribly supportive, but that's okay. Everyone has a strange uncle who leers awkwardly or a smug cousin who can't see beyond his next purchase. But that doesn't matter too much...

You see the problem? It's possible to have one or more close relationships within your family, but it's also very likely (even expected) to have at least one person who qualifies as family to whom you don't feel close at all. Most of us have a number of family relationships that, if stripped of the "family" title, would not be worth maintaining. An unfortunate few have nobody in their family who makes them feel anything other than judged, ridiculed, or misunderstood.

So what makes some family relationships work for reducing loneliness and others not? Before we get to that, let's take a step back and consider the simplest of questions: Who exactly *is* our family? If you think that's a silly question, you likely have a mother, father, and some siblings. But if you have two moms or two dads, you've probably thought about this. Or if you've adopted a child or been adopted yourself. Or if you're estranged from your family.

According to Mary Jo Maynes, author of *The Family*, there is no natural or predetermined definition for who is and who isn't family: "Different societies have different definitions of who counts as family members; in some societies your mother's second cousin is a kinsman of note, while in others (such as our own) many people cannot even name their mother's second cousins."

We know that family is not just genetic relationships. A single parent with an adopted baby is recognized as full family under the law. And we know it's not just legal relationships, either. A couple who's been together for twenty years and has three kids but never filed the marriage paperwork is considered family from most modern perspectives.

So what makes a family *a family?*

Let's try on a few ideas for size. Maybe a family is a group of people who form bonds because they live together — because they share a *home.* Cohabitation is important enough to the idea of family that Maynes includes it in her formal definition of the term: "Families are small groups of people linked by culturally recognized ties of marriage or similar forms of partnership, descent, and/or adoption, who typically share a household for some period of time."

But according to a 2008 Pew Social & Demographic Trends survey: "Home means different things to different people. Among U.S.-born adults who have lived in more than one community, nearly four-in-ten (38%) say the place they consider home isn't where they're living now... 26% say it's where they were born or raised; 22% say it's where they live now; 18% say it's where they have lived the longest; 15% say it's where their family comes from; and 4% say it's where they went to high school." These widely varying perceptions of home make clear that cohabitation is not fundamentally what makes family *family.*

Could it be that family is defined by mutual responsibilities? Parents take care of their children and, when they grow up, children take care of their parents. Maybe. But one booming industry begs to differ. In January 2014, a company called Care.com went public after raising $111 million in venture funding. As the preeminent "care marketplace," Care.com "offers solutions to help families make informed decisions in one of the most important and highly considered aspects of their family life — finding and managing quality care for their family."

Whatever feelings it may stir to think about hiring someone to care for your loved ones, the reality is that we now have the opportunity to outsource many of our traditional family duties. We don't *have* to look out for one another in the same way we once did — there simply aren't the same consequences there once were — and I'm convinced that simple obligation is not what makes a family *a family*.

My belief is that family is fundamentally a feeling...and that feeling is closeness. Closeness is what makes family *feel like family*. Without closeness, our relationships with our family members feel just as bad (or even worse, owing to our heightened expectations) as any other set of relationships that lack knowing and caring.

In the introduction, I mentioned that most people think there are many different kinds of relationships, but in fact all relationships lie somewhere on a single spectrum from distant to close. This means any relationship can be close, but it also means any relationship can be distant. Just because someone is your mother, father, sister, or brother does not mean your relationship with him or her will not be on the distant end of the spectrum.

No relationships — regardless of title — are intrinsically closer than others. All require the efforts of knowing and caring. Family members certainly *can* feel close, but only if they put in the effort.

That being said, family does have some unique advantages in creating closeness, particularly in the area of knowing. Your family members have the potential to know you well because of your extensive shared history and shared experiences. There are few people outside of family with whom you will spend as much time over the course of your life, especially during your formative years. This access to one another over long periods of time (and at different stages of life) is a real opportunity. If the opportunity is seized on and used in the efforts of deep knowing, family can be an excellent source of closeness.

But family also has one great disadvantage: complacency. Family members, more so than any other people in relationships, tend to think they don't have to do anything to maintain the relationship. "Family is forever," right? While this can be a deeply comforting thought, don't let it become an excuse not to try. Don't let "family is forever" get translated into "I don't have to be nice to you because you couldn't get rid of me even if you tried."

Family may be forever, but the *feeling of family* — closeness — is not forever without active, sustained effort.

Myth 2: Some types of relationships are inherently closer than others.

Myth 2 reframed: Any relationship can be close, and any relationship can be distant.

Myth 3: If You're Lonely, Just Be Around People

Of all the myths about what reduces loneliness, this one is the stickiest. Does it feel good to be around others when you're lonely? The answer is a resounding *sometimes*. If you go to a social gathering and make a spontaneous new friend, it's the best. If you go and feel out of place, ostracized, or just…awkward, it can be the worst.

So let's just get this out of the way: the obvious reason why having people around isn't a good solution to our contemporary loneliness is that it's terribly, painfully unpredictable.

But *why* is it so unpredictable? Why is it so unlike the stale loaf of bread vs. the fresh one — both of which achieve the same goal of reducing hunger? What I've found is that we make a subtle but important mistake in our quest to be around people: we don't distinguish between people who are around us *for us* and people who are around us because of the situation.

I use the term *situational proximity* to describe the experience of having people around you because of the context, not because you necessarily want to be around one another. This can mean living in an apartment with four roommates, sitting in a class of five hundred people, or working in an office of thousands. Situational proximity means there are people (often lots of people) around you physically, but they are there for reasons other than being near you.

Situational proximity is a big — and little acknowledged — part of why being around people is so unpredictable when it comes to reducing loneliness. If you and another person haven't gotten together for the purpose of being together, it's totally up in the air how that person will make you feel. If you start chatting with a girl in class with the goal of feeling less lonely, and she chats back with the goal of understanding the class material better, you're likely not going to walk away with your goal met. These difference in goals — differences in *intentions* — can be highly discouraging for someone looking to be less lonely.

That being said, there is always a chance that meeting up with someone who *is* there to meet up with you won't make you feel all that great either. But it's much more likely that the other person will try. At the very least, your intentions are aligned. It's much more likely she'll put in the effort and be engaged with you — usually making for a much more satisfying interaction.

And it's that feeling — the satisfying feeling of being with someone who wants to know you and who cares to engage — that alleviates loneliness. As you've probably guessed, the feeling that makes being around people pay off is closeness.

This difference between situational proximity and the experience of closeness can be seen most clearly in working environments. Working environments are inherently situational — everyone is really there to work (and to get paid, of course), not because they like everyone around them. This begs the question "Does having people around at work generally make someone who struggles with loneliness more or less lonely?"

It would stand to reason that a larger work team would mean more opportunities to create closeness. There would be more people to try on for size and see whom you're drawn to as a potential closeness partner. But does this actually pan out?

I was particularly curious about this question because Silicon Valley has a very strong inclination toward keeping work teams small. Jeff Bezos, founder of Amazon.com, famously said that when you can no longer feed a team with two pizzas, it has gotten too big. I wondered if this was simply the technology mind-set coming into play, since smaller teams are often more efficient. But this bias toward smaller teams seems to be about more than just efficiency. Research supports the idea that larger teams make people *feel worse* — specifically, more alienated from one another.

Psychologist Jennifer Mueller coined the term *relational loss* to describe the experience of feeling lonelier the more people you work with. Based on her 2012 study, which examined 212 employees in twenty-six teams, ranging from three to nineteen members, Mueller discovered that each employee becomes less engaged at work as team size increases. She theorized that this occurs because as team size gets bigger, each individual perceives that less support is available.

Support in this context may mean practical support, that is, training and feedback. But it surely also means the other kind of support as well — the emotional and psychological awareness that others around you care.

As Mueller put it: "[I]n these larger teams, people were lost. They didn't know who to call for help because they didn't know the other members well enough. Even if they did reach out, they didn't feel the other members were as committed to helping or had the time to help. And they couldn't tell their team leader because [it would look like] they had failed." If this doesn't describe distance caused by a lack of knowing and caring, I don't know what does.

Moreover, when a team suffers a knowing and caring deficit, it appears that employees don't just become more distant from one other; they also become more distant from the work itself. A survey published by Gallup showed that "employee engagement is broken down by company size, the smallest companies have the most engaged employees — and it [isn't] even close. 42% of employees working at small companies of ten and fewer reported that they were engaged at work, a huge increase over the 27% to 30% of engaged people at larger companies."

This disconnect between having people around and still feeling isolated is all about perceptions. It's not a physical loneliness, but a loneliness of the heart and mind. It's the new kind of loneliness creeping in. If you perceive that most of your coworkers know you and care about you, it may not matter how big your team is. But the smaller your team, the more likely it is that your colleagues will know you and care about you.

In other words, it's not the number of hours you spend working on a project together. It's not the number of emails you exchange or the number of meetings you attend together. Feeling integrated with those around you is really all about closeness — even at the workplace.

To start reducing loneliness in situational contexts like work, I recommend using proximity to others in service of creating closeness. Here's one way to do that: use the recurring nature of work — seeing the same people every day — to get to know others gradually. Work is a low-pressure environment in terms of creating closeness (as opposed to a date, for example, where there's more pressure to decide quickly if you like each other) and gives you the benefit of time. Feel people out, pick those you feel drawn to, and build closeness at a comfortable pace. Start with a chat in passing, and work up to getting coffee together before a meeting, for example. This process can, over time, make your office one of your favorite places to be!

Myth 3: If you're lonely, just be around people.

Myth 3 reframed: Being around people can reduce or increase loneliness, depending on how those people make you feel — close to them, or distant.

Questions for Reflection

- How have your love relationships affected how lonely you feel? Have they made you feel more or less lonely?
- Which member of your family would you like to get closer to? Who would you like to let go of?
- Are there other relationship myths you would like to reexamine through the lens of closeness? What might they look like?

 ## An Exercise to Challenge Yourself

Which type of relationship do you tend to look toward to feel less lonely? Do you call your parents when you feel lonely? Do you go on dates looking for love? For two weeks, put this habit aside and turn your efforts toward creating closeness in another area of your life. Instead of calling on family members, cultivate some work relationships. Instead of going on dates, put more energy into your friendships.

Chapter Summary

Of all the myths about what "solves" loneliness, the three most problematic ones are:

1. **Love is a reliable solution to loneliness.** Love certainly reduces loneliness, given the right circumstances, but it can also increase loneliness. Closeness, unlike love, always works toward reducing loneliness. Closeness is *useful* in a way that love is not. **Myth 1 reframed: Love is a mystery; closeness is not.**

2. **Some types of relationships are inherently closer than others.** In fact, where a relationship falls on the spectrum from distant to close is a product of the mutual efforts of knowing and caring. No relationship (or type of relationship) is "supposed" to reduce loneliness. **Myth 2 reframed: Any relationship can be close, and any relationship can be distant.**

3. **If you're lonely, just be around people.** Having people around does not in and of itself solve loneliness. What fills an interaction with a sense of satisfaction and happiness is how you make each other feel. **Myth 3 reframed: Being around people can reduce or increase loneliness, depending on how those people make you feel — close or distant.**

Try to relinquish these outdated notions about what "should" reduce loneliness. These myths will trip you up if you don't put them to the side.

Chapter 4

Learning to Pick Partners

M y favorite social experiment in learning to pick partners can't be found in any social science literature. Instead, it can be found on your TV, Monday nights at 8:00 PM. It's called *The Bachelor*.

For those who don't know, *The Bachelor* provides one man — the eponymous bachelor — a group of twenty-five to thirty gorgeous women from whom he must choose a wife. Not a girlfriend, a wife. The goal of the show is to turn the bachelor into a married man.

The Bachelor is absolutely brilliant...just not at making marriages. According to *Wikipedia*, as of March 2015 only five marriages have come out of the twenty-nine seasons of *The Bachelor* and its gender-reverse counterpart, *The Bachelorette*, combined. But the show *is* genius at a particular aspect of relationships: making people *think they're falling in love*.

How does the show do this? It's easy to chalk it up to everyone being ridiculously good-looking, plus the impossibly romantic, expense-free dates. Rappelling down the highest cliff in Bali and then attending a private concert by the biggest local pop star, anyone? Swimming in a cove of endangered dolphins and then dining in a thousand-year-old castle? A little adrenaline, a little romance, and everyone's in love!

But we all know it's not that simple. Love is a mystery...but it's not a conjuring act.

Perhaps everyone on the show believes they're falling in love because they really *want* to be in love. The people who apply to be on the show are certainly a self-selected bunch. If you're not looking for the experience of love and potentially marriage, there's little reason to go on the show in the first place. Is it simply wish fulfillment?

Maybe. But one night as my husband (who good-naturedly tolerates it) and I sat watching the show, he made an intriguing comment. "Why doesn't that girl just leave? She doesn't like the bachelor at all. They have nothing in common."

This gave me pause. In fact, the women almost never leave — they only depart when the bachelor rejects them. On very few occasions has a woman left simply because she wasn't feeling it. But sometimes it's glaringly obvious that a particular woman on the show is a bad match for the bachelor. Why *doesn't* she just leave?

Her answer is always simple: "I think I could be falling in love!" "I think he could be my husband...we have such a strong connection...I want to see where this goes!" And this, right here, is what the show gets right. This is why *The Bachelor* is brilliant. Out of the vast pantheon of feelings, the show has distilled the specific feeling of *attraction*. It knows that attraction is vital in budding relationships and has learned to evoke it in complete strangers. Attraction is, in fact, the starting point of *all* close relationships.

As I define it, attraction is the energy of potential with another person. It is the feeling of being interested in someone, the feeling that this might be something great. *The Bachelor* may be frivolous, but attraction is not. Attraction is the first draw toward someone else...the first step closer.

The Draw toward Others

It's a misconception that people who struggle with loneliness don't feel drawn toward others. Most lonely people are not recluses or innate "lone wolves." Most *do* meet people they like — people they admire or find interesting. The breakdown in connection often happens in the transition from being interested to getting close.

It's this interest — this attraction — that's the starting point for all close relationships. The word *attraction* unfortunately feels like it belongs solely to the realm of romance; we usually hear it in the context of physical attraction. But attraction simply means the experience of feeling drawn to someone — feeling interested in getting to know him or her better.

While the romantic versions of attraction — lust and infatuation — can certainly be a starting point for closeness with romantic partners, attraction has a much broader scope. Let's say you're in grad school and feel drawn to a particular professor's intellect. That's attraction. Or you've just attended your first company meeting and feel compelled to know more about the CEO's backstory. That's attraction too.

Attraction is essentially your intuition assessing the situation before your conscious mind gets the chance to. Attraction is your subconscious picking up on subtle cues that it likes before your conscious mind understands exactly *what it is* it's liking. I find evidence for this in the fact that attraction is often described as a spiritual or psychic experience, as a meeting of the minds or a melding of hearts. Love at first sight. Instant connection.

Attraction is simply a finger pointing toward potential closeness.

A former client of mine who worked at a very large company — we'll call him Julian — struggled to manage a strained relationship with his boss. He found his boss much too harsh. It wasn't necessarily the critical feedback that bothered him — Julian simply didn't like the tone in which his boss spoke to him. It was flippant, dismissive. Unfortunately, Julian felt his working environment wouldn't allow for him to simply ask someone to be nicer.

As I worked with Julian to improve his relationship with his boss, I felt we were making little headway. Until, that is, I asked him this: "So, your boss doesn't speak to you in a way you like. Who *does* speak to you in a way you like?"

He paused. A smile spread across his face.

"This is random," Julian began, "but this one time I was in a restaurant with my wife and the waiter kept calling us 'my friends.' 'More water, my friends?' 'Do you want ketchup, my friends?' It sounds cheesy, but it wasn't. He meant it. Everyone was his friend."

That, my friends, is attraction. Julian was attracted to the waiter's friendliness and openness. It was the smallest, simplest moment of meeting someone and thinking, "I like you!" Eventually, Julian came to the conclusion that he needed to be around people who were friendlier and more open, and he moved to a much smaller company.

Julian's story demonstrates that there's no reason why attraction can't exist — as a powerful force, no less — in all realms, including friendship, family, and professional. Attraction is much more universal than we think. But how do you transition from meeting someone and feeling attracted to getting to know him?

Let's look at Julian's situation. He could have done a few things to initiate *knowing* with the waiter he liked. He could have:

- Come back to the restaurant another day and chatted with the waiter again
- Made up a pretense for planning to get together, perhaps under the guise of doing business together
- Made a straightforward statement that he liked how the waiter carried himself and would like to get to know him better

Do these advances sound odd...or even scary? They likely do. Which brings us to the final option. Julian could have done nothing — which is indeed what he did, and most of us would have done the same. It's quite common to feel uncomfortable approaching someone with the intention of getting closer. But the thing to remember is that these *really are* the opportunities that lead to closeness. Opportunities can be large — like a lifelong bond with a sibling — or they can be very small — like a chance encounter with a friendly waiter.

Once you start looking at your environment through the lens of closeness, you'll notice that these opportunities are all around you. Attraction springs up spontaneously. You might meet a new person or suddenly start seeing an old person in a new light. Attraction happens when it happens. Your job is to be brave and to seize the opportunity.

Knowing at First Sight

The unique quality that makes attraction a great starting point for finding partners — its feeling of potential — is also its biggest stumbling block. Attraction has great energetic power; it can feel like the pull of gravity. It's not uncommon to hear someone say they were drawn to another person like a magnet. Attraction is exciting, no doubt, but its energy can also yank people right into a full-blown relationship before they've actually gotten to know each other.

When it comes to picking partners, start with attraction. But don't *stop* with attraction.

A strong attraction makes it very easy to jump to conclusions, to fill in the blanks of who the other person is with your own assumptions. She started her own company, so she must have her head screwed on straight! He's a single dad, so he must be really loving and affectionate! Well...you don't really know that yet.

It takes some time and effort — detailed in the chapters on knowing — to get to know someone on a deep enough level to call it closeness. For now you need to hold fast to the reality that even if you really like this person, you don't really *know* her yet. In other words, love at first sight may be real, but "knowing at first sight" is not. Knowing at first sight is at best wishful thinking. At worst, it's a recipe for serious disappointment. Don't let yourself get close to a fantasy.

You may be thinking, "I never do this. I know the difference between fantasy and reality." But evidence shows that we start constructing our idea of who another person is on first contact. Just one picture on Tinder, one tweet we find hilarious or off-putting, and we think we know who the person is.

As *The Bachelor* proves, no activity is more ruled by fantasies than dating. Researcher Artemio Ramirez, who conducted a study of online daters to determine if the amount of time spent talking online affected real-life outcomes, found that the image we create in our heads about another person is a truly powerful force:

> The results of the present study suggest online daters create mental constructs of their potential partners by reading their online dating profile, using that information to fill-in-the-blanks of who the partner might really be in the offline world. Daters who wait too long to meet in

person, and therefore cross this tipping point, might find it difficult to accept any discrepancies from their idealized mental construct of their partner. Crossing the tipping point should be particularly harmful for daters who developed very inaccurate partner expectations due to the partner's use of dishonesty, misrepresentation, or even exaggeration on their profile.

So how do you cross this threshold from attraction to knowing while avoiding the stumbling block of assuming? How do you successfully navigate the waters of liking-but-not-really-knowing-for-sure?

This is one of the biggest challenges you'll face in your journey out of loneliness. Because the first few encounters in a new relationship can be a very uncertain time, I encourage you to hit a few specific notes before committing to pursuing someone as a closeness partner. If you miss any of these notes, there's a chance you may be moving too fast from attraction to full-blown relationship. (And remember, this applies to all types of relationships, not just romantic ones.)

The notes I encourage you to hit when first trying on a new friend, family member, colleague, or romantic partner are:

1. Identify attractions.

2. Meet in person. If it's a romantic relationship, feel free to ask him or her on a date. If it's a business relationship, grab coffee together.

3. Ask a few deeper questions. Later in this book you will learn how to ask deep questions. But for now, simply make an effort to probe a little deeper. If your boss talks about enjoying sailing, ask, "What do you like about it?" If your acquaintance is interviewing for a new job, ask, "What do you want out of the job?"

4. Assess for certain skills. You're not looking for any "right" or "wrong" answers to your deeper questions; you're looking for *skills that indicate whether or not this person will be good at knowing and caring.*

Let's discuss these skills in detail. The first four indicate proficiency in knowing; the second four indicate proficiency in caring. Let's tackle the four knowing skills first.

Skill 1: The Ability to Self-Disclose

The ability to self-disclose essentially means being willing to reveal parts of one's inner world to someone else. It wouldn't be an exaggeration to say that this is *the* fundamental ability required in creating closeness. At its core, self-disclosing means openness and honesty, as well as a desire to share a range of information about oneself — both factual and subjective.

A factual disclosure could be as simple as revealing you're from Michigan. A subjective disclosure would include telling the other person how you *feel* about being from Michigan. What was your favorite part of growing up there? Do you like going back?

These subjective disclosures can be easy to overlook, since we're trained from school and work situations to focus on remembering the facts. While the facts are important, the feelings behind the facts are more important in creating closeness. Most people will tell anyone where they're from. But they will only tell a potential confidante how they *feel* about where they're from.

As well-known social psychologist Harry Reis described in his theory of intimacy: "Although factual and emotional self-disclosures reveal personal information about oneself, emotional self-disclosures are considered to be more closely related to the experience of intimacy because they allow for the most core aspects of the self to be known, understood, and validated."

Things to Notice

- Does he avoid answering personal questions?
- Does he create factual inconsistencies or tell full-blown lies?
- Does he use deflection or humor to avoid certain subjects?

Skill 2: The Ability to Reciprocate

The ability to reciprocate, as I define it, means being able both to give someone their moment and to take your own moment. Stated another way, it is the ability to let someone else be the focus (at certain moments) and also to let yourself be the focus (at other moments). The ability to reciprocate in this way matters because if one person in the relationship is always the center of attention, neglect and inequality become inevitable.

Those who struggle with reciprocating tend to gather at opposite ends of the spectrum: they are either very self-centered or very self-effacing. Neither of these extremes works well for creating closeness. An ideal partner would see interactions as something of a tennis match — lobbing the focus over to you and then actively swinging at it when it comes back her way.

Things to Notice

- Does she hog the conversation or talk as if you're not there?
- Does she send a barrage of questions your way but answer few in return?
- Does the conversation feel forced?

Skill 3: The Ability to Accept New Information

Specifically, this means the other person should be able to accept new information about you. Early on, it's natural for a person to develop a picture of who they think you are, but problems arise if that early picture becomes fixed. For closeness to flourish, the person you are getting to know must be able to reevaluate and reformulate his ideas about you regularly. In other words, if you reveal more about yourself over time yet find he doesn't believe you because these disclosures don't match his early idea of you, that's a problem. That's a red flag that he's falling for a fantasy of you.

Anybody with whom you choose to create closeness should be able to let go of the mental construct of you he created before he knew you well.

Things to Notice

- Does he retain new information about you?
- Does he try to talk you out of what you're saying about yourself?
- Is he making sweeping assumptions about you?

Skill 4: The Ability to Be Present

The ability to be present means being in the moment, focused on what's happening here and now. It can be as simple as disconnecting from personal technology and giving full attention to your partner. But being present means much more than just being able to put down a phone. It means being willing to change with each moment.

In other words, a partner who is fixated on what has been in the past or what will be in the future is just that — fixated. She's weighed down with baggage. She's stuck in some other place and time...somewhere you can't go. If you can't both be here and now, closeness is unlikely to grow. Fundamentally, you will achieve knowing and caring through lots of little moments of being present with each other.

Things to Notice

- Does she make eye contact — one of the primary indicators of present engagement?
- Does she tend to redirect the conversation to past or future events?
- Does she use language that casts the conversations in the past or future — using words such as *then* and *there* instead of *now* and *here*?

Now let's tackle the four caring skills.

Skill 1: The Ability to Feel and Express Emotions

This one is pretty self-explanatory. It's impossible to get close to someone who either cannot feel feelings or cannot express them. Whether the other person is actually *feeling* can be very hard to determine from casual conversation, so I recommend focusing on whether she can express emotion.

Look for feeling language of any kind. "I love when this happens..." "I hate when I can't..." Pay particular attention to any caring language around other people in her life. One sincere expression of love for another person in her life is an excellent sign.

Things to Notice

- Does he use feeling language?
- Does he use facial expressions and gestures to convey emotion?
- Does he have a flat affect or seem robotic?

Skill 2: The Ability to Respond Appropriately

The ability to respond appropriately is similar to the ability to reciprocate. It's about being able to notice when your partner needs your attention and then giving her that attention. To respond appropriately is to give someone her moment on an emotional level.

As the social psychology literature describes, "Intimacy is initiated when one person communicates personally relevant and revealing information, thoughts, and feelings to another person. For intimacy processes to continue, the listener must emit emotions, expressions, and behaviors that are both responsive to the specific content of the disclosure and convey acceptance, validation, and caring for the individual disclosing. For the interaction to be experienced as intimate by the discloser, he or she must subjectively feel understood, validated, and cared for."

This skill matters because picking someone who can respond to you appropriately is ultimately what will make *you* feel cared about in the relationship.

Things to Notice

- Does she respond emotionally in a way that feels good, such as holding your hand when you're expressing fear or concern?
- Does she respond emotionally in a way that feels bad, such as laughing while you tell the story of your dying grandparent?

Skill 3: The Ability to Take Responsibility

The ability to take responsibility means owning your actions and decisions. It doesn't mean inviting blame for everything that's going on around you, but it does include recognizing the part you played in creating a bad situation.

Personal responsibility is absolutely essential in making great relationships. Things *will* go wrong, no matter how hard you try, and it's critical to pick someone who will feel some ownership over what went wrong. If not, you'll end up with all the blame... and blame is a major closeness killer.

Things to Notice

- Does he blame other people or outside circumstances for his disappointments?
- Does he bad-mouth current or past bosses, spouses, partners, and so on?
- Is he unable to apologize sincerely?

Skill 4: The Ability to Accept Caring

Have you ever heard the saying "In every relationship, one person is the flower and the other is the gardener"? There's probably nothing I find less true. Caring — in the closeness sense of the word — is not the same as care-taking. Getting close to someone does not mean signing up to be his or her nurse or rescuer; nor does it mean signing up only to receive care. You will both need to be the flower, and both be the gardener.

The caring abilities listed above should prove a potential partner's ability to give you the care you need. This one is about making sure he or she can receive care. If your potential partner shuns your caring — for example, "not wanting to talk about it" when you offer to listen — this is a difficult barrier to overcome when creating closeness.

Things to Notice

- Does she allow you to support her emotionally?
- Does she seem stoic or reluctant to reveal anything too private?
- Is she unwilling to admit her vulnerabilities?

When you see the hallmarks of someone capable of knowing *and* caring — get excited! This is a great opportunity. This person will likely make a wonderful partner. The rest of this book will show you how to establish a wonderful relationship.

But if, as often happens, you find that though your potential partner has many of these abilities locked down, a few are still lacking — don't give up. These abilities can be learned over time, especially if you lead by example. Be patient, and recognize that she may need some practice before becoming proficient at creating closeness.

Red Flags

Keep in mind that while you're testing the closeness waters you absolutely do not need to create closeness with every person you meet in order to reduce your loneliness. Remember — becoming just a little closer to one or two people will ease the pangs of feeling alone. In other words, there's no need to force it. If you have reservations about someone, give it some time, or resolve to simply let that opportunity go. Trust that there will be other opportunities, because there will be.

Here I want to note that there are some people whom you really should not try to get closer to. Some of these partners are inappropriate simply because of the situation. For example, it could be seen as inappropriate to make an effort to get close to a friend's spouse. These are judgment calls — some actions could be seen as overstepping boundaries by some and as perfectly fine by others.

Just be aware of how picking this partner or that might make those around you feel.

Other inappropriate partners will be poor at creating closeness with you, not because of the situation, but because of their basic personality traits. Two of these personality profiles are well known to be dangerous, regardless of the context: the sociopath and the psychopath.

Because the terms *sociopath* and *psychopath* are very loaded and often misunderstood, it may be easier to identify these two types of dangerous people based on the descriptions outlined by research psychologists John and Julie Gottman. They categorize the two most dangerous personality types as "pit bulls" and "cobras."

Pit bulls tend to show:

- Explosive anger
- Suspicion, distrust, and jealousy
- A lecturing or condescending attitude
- Violent tendencies that build over time and are directed at those closest to them

Cobras tend to show:

- A charming exterior
- Manipulative behavior
- An enjoyment of watching fear build in others
- Violent tendencies that usually come as a surprise and can be directed at anyone

For obvious reasons, people displaying these clusters of personality traits should be avoided at all costs. Who else should be avoided? Because closeness partners will be given so much access to your inner world — in a sense, so much power — if there's any personality trait or characteristic you absolutely cannot tolerate, you should make it a deal breaker. While the pit bull and cobra personality types are universal deal breakers, it's a great idea to come up with your own.

Here are some of the deal breakers I have been told about over the years:

- A sober woman decided not to partner with a friend who drinks. Drinking became a deal breaker for her, and she is now close only with those who are also sober.
- A man who was raised by a very depressed mom decided not to pursue a woman he was attracted to because she also struggled with depression.
- A single dad decided not to get close to a fellow single dad at work because he constantly criticized and denounced his children's mother. In his eyes, this behavior was a deal breaker.

How do you know if something is a deal breaker for you? It usually helps to check in with yourself about your past. Have you experienced something with a previous partner that you absolutely will not allow for again? That's definitely a deal breaker.

Also, use your intuition. Do you find yourself feeling uneasy around a certain person? Do you feel a creeping anxiety when you're on your way to see him or her? These seemingly baseless reactions probably mean something. Does his humor sting a little too much? Is her competitiveness turning you off? These are the things to notice. These are the seeds of deal breakers.

Picking closeness partners is a personal journey. Not everyone will be attracted to the same people. Allow yourself to be drawn to whomever makes you feel the most seen and understood. These are your closest companions in the making.

Questions for Reflection

- Of all the people you know, who seems the most proficient at the four essential knowing skills? The four essential caring skills?

- Are there any people in your life who are inappropriate closeness partners, either because of the situation or because of their character traits?
- What are some of your deal breakers when it comes to picking partners? What are some qualities you absolutely must (or must not) have in someone you want to be close to?

 ## An Exercise to Challenge Yourself

Jot down a list of all the people you've met this year. Pick one person you'd like to know better. Make the first move, and ask him or her to hang out!

Chapter Summary

- Attraction is the first impetus toward closeness. It's the feeling of being drawn to someone — not just in the realm of romance but in all realms. It's the desire to get to know someone better. Attraction is the starting point for picking partners; it usually arises spontaneously.
- When you're moving past attraction into your first attempts at getting to know someone, you're looking for her to have certain abilities that indicate she's capable of creating closeness with someone.
- The four skills of someone capable of knowing are:
  1. The ability to self-disclose
  2. The ability to reciprocate moments
  3. The ability to accept new information
  4. The ability to be present

- The four skills of someone who is capable of caring are:
  1. The ability to feel and express emotions
  2. The ability to respond appropriately
  3. The ability to take personal responsibility
  4. The ability to accept caring from others

- Remember that you do not have to create closeness with everyone you meet. Some people — "cobras" and "pit bulls" — would be bad matches for everyone. It's also reasonable to reject a potential partner based on your requirements — your deal breakers.

Part 2

Mastering
the Art of
Knowing

Chapter 5

Gaining Access to Another Person's World

In the last few chapters you learned what closeness is and how it chases away loneliness. You learned about the benefits of close relationships and the obstacles we all face in finding them. You've let go of some unhelpful myths about what reduces loneliness, and you've learned how to pick partners. Now it's time to dive into learning how to create closeness with another person.

The first step in experiencing closeness is, as we know, mastering the art of knowing. True and deep knowing means understanding another person from that person's perspective. So how does one develop this ability in a methodical and reliable way?

Before we go into the mechanics of knowing another person well, let's address a basic question: Why do we need to *learn* to do this? Or, stated another way, what's preventing us from achieving this type of deep knowing already?

For most of us who struggle with feeling lonely, knowing another person very well — and feeling known in return — is a pretty rare occurrence. Deep, close relationships are few and far between. It usually takes a significant amount of time for both people to open up. If asked after a dinner date how much we knew about the person with whom we'd just dined, most of us would say we knew hardly anything.

Why is this? What makes it difficult to get to know people deeply yet efficiently? When I've posed this question to my clients who struggle with loneliness, most of them say they need to establish a certain level of trust with another person before they feel comfortable opening up. The desire to not hand over too much information — too much power — to a relative stranger is perfectly reasonable. This protective stance serves us pretty well most of the time.

But if closeness is our goal, and we feel drawn to another person and see no red flags...why do we still hold back? My perspective is that we are not actually holding back. We are no longer trying to protect ourselves; we simply don't know how to talk to each other in a way that helps us access each other's inner worlds.

This is the stage at which we get stuck. We get stuck talking about what we did that day. We get stuck reciting summaries of what we're working on and what we're doing in our spare time. We get stuck discussing our new phones or our new purses. We get stuck talking about trivialities. We get stuck talking about *wants*.

These surface-level conversations — the types that focus primarily on wants — are very common and not particularly helpful in getting to know someone well. Let's start to understand what these conversations look like, and why we need to get unstuck.

The Want-Assume-Misunderstand Cycle

What do I really mean by conversations that focus on "wants?" The wants I'm referring to here are things about you that you wouldn't mind telling anyone. For example, you'd likely tell just about anyone what you like to do on weekends ("I want to go golfing") or what type of wine you like best ("I want a Cabernet").

Even information that seems to go a bit deeper — such as telling someone that you'd like to change careers or that you want to buy a house — still rests on the surface level of knowing someone.

Take the example of wanting to buy a house. You're out with a new friend and tell her you're looking to buy a house. She's interested — she's always wanted to own her own home too. Since this is a very common want (lots of people feel a desire to buy a house), it's easy for your friend to assume that your reason for wanting the house is the same as hers. She walks away thinking, "We're both at the same place in life. We have a lot in common!"

But here's the catch. When you scratch the surface of the want, you'll find there are innumerable possible reasons for wanting to buy a house. Here are just a few reasons a person could give:

- "I value long-term investments, and a house is a great investment."
- "I'd like the stability that comes with putting down roots."
- "I've had one too many terrible landlords. I need the freedom of my own space!"
- "I've always dreamed of designing and decorating a house from top to bottom."
- "My kids deserve to stop moving every few years."
- "I'm mostly just looking to fix the place up and turn a profit."
- "All my friends own their own homes — I want to be in the club!"

You see the problem? It's not that your reason for wanting to buy a house might be different from your new friend's reason. Differences are not closeness killers. The problem is that the underlying reason for the want was left completely out of the conversation, leaving the want itself to tell the whole story. And wants are *not* the whole story.

Imagine your friend's surprise when you indeed buy a house and then quickly flip it. She was envisioning the two of you being neighbors! How perplexing for her to find that her expectations were totally wrong. If it had been a more serious misunderstanding, she could walk away thinking, "Wow, I really don't know her at all!"

You may be thinking, "Asking someone why she wants to buy a house is great, but not every want is all that deep." That's true. Sometimes wanting to get a haircut has no deeper meaning than wanting to prevent your bangs from falling in your eyes.

The issue here is that collectively we have become practiced at *not* investigating wants, and often we miss opportunities to get closer. Maybe your friend wants a haircut because her bangs keep falling in her eyes, but maybe she wants a haircut because she wants to reinvent herself. You really don't know until you ask.

Our habit of not investigating wants is a real problem when it comes to getting to know one another. Wants are very rarely an endgame in and of themselves. It's usually not as simple as "When I get the thing I want, I will be satisfied." Wants are more often than not a finger pointing toward something deeper. If that deeper component is never addressed or never invited to show itself, how can you gain access to another person's inner world?

Sharing a want with another person — such as wanting to buy a house — *does* mean you have something in common. But if that want is never investigated, it's easy to assume you also have that deeper component in common, which can lead to fundamental misunderstandings about each other. This breakdown in knowing is what I call the Want-Assume-Misunderstand cycle.

Let's look at an example of this cycle in action.

Amy and Alex were adult siblings who had always had a very playful relationship. They rarely saw each other because they lived in different cities, but when they met up for holidays and birthdays, they teased each other as if they were kids again.

One Thanksgiving, Alex and his wife, Elizabeth, showed up to family dinner with a new puppy. Everyone in the family fawned over it — most of all Amy. She played with it all afternoon and couldn't stop talking about how fun it would be to come home every day to this kind of excitement.

By the time Christmas rolled around, Amy had adopted her own puppy, whom she debuted with fanfare at their family's Christmas Eve dinner. Alex — ever the big brother — started teasing her relentlessly about getting the puppy. But to her surprise, his teasing took an odd turn: he was mostly teasing her about having "baby fever." Amy, confused and a bit unnerved, pulled Alex into a bedroom to talk.

"Why are you talking about babies?" she confronted him. "What does that have to do with anything?"

"Well, that's why Elizabeth and I got a dog...to practice for when we have babies," he replied sheepishly.

They looked at each other.

"I JUST THINK DOGS ARE FUN, YOU IDIOT!" Amy cried.

It was so silly they both had to laugh. Luckily for Amy and Alex, this was an innocuous presentation of the Want-Assume-Misunderstand cycle. But you can see how this degree of misunderstanding — essentially being *completely wrong* about someone else's motivations for doing something — can be very divisive. If the misunderstanding is about anything of importance, it's one of the most distance-creating mistakes you can make.

When we make assumptions, we're really filling in someone else's depth with a projection of our own depths. We don't actually gain access to the other person's inner world; we see a reflection of our own inner world. Assumptions produce surface-level relationships at best. At worst, they produce highly unstable relationships that are prone to self-destruction.

An example of how the Want-Assume-Misunderstand cycle can create unstable relationships exists in the life story of one of the most famous people of our age: Kim Kardashian.

In October 2011 Kim Kardashian filed for divorce from basketball player Kris Humphries after just seventy-two days of marriage. The wedding — which had reportedly cost around $10 million — was showcased over four installments on her E! TV show *Keeping Up with the Kardashians*. This combination of an extravagantly showcased wedding and a hastily concluded divorce drew much ire from the public. Many thought it was a stunt, fiction, or all-out fraud.

I, for one, was convinced it was a real marriage based on love but one in which the spouses had simply never discussed their lives beyond their wants. She seemed to want to marry a high-profile athlete. He was a high-profile athlete. She wanted to have kids. He too wanted to have kids. She wanted to have a Christian household. He too wanted to have a Christian household. Perfect match, right?

Seems not. I'd suspect they both truly believed they had vetted each other well before deciding to marry — which I'm guessing made the divorce even more shocking when it came. The problem is that Kim and Kris fell into a classic trap — a version of the Want-Assume-Misunderstand cycle found in romantic relationships — called "Do we want the same things?"

Figuring out if a potential spouse wants what you want is a great place to start...but it's just a place *to start*. The more important part comes next: investigating what these respective wants really mean. For example, what does wanting to marry a high-profile athlete *mean*? Does it mean access to wealth? Does it mean not having to work? Does it mean she just likes sports?

It turns out that what "marrying a high-profile athlete" meant to Kim — as revealed on one of the other Kardashian shows, *Kourtney and Kim Take New York* — was support in her career as a professional famous person. Unfortunately, she soon found out that Kris's wants meant almost exactly the opposite. He thought she intended to give up her career and be a wife and a mom.

Watching this story unfold, it was hard for me not to feel bad for Kim. In a handful of scenes, you can see the realization sweep across her face: I made too many assumptions. He wants something *completely different*. I thought we wanted the same things! I thought we discussed this! But really, they didn't. They discussed their wants; she filled in the deeper meaning of those wants with what they meant to her, and he filled in the deeper meaning of those wants with what they meant to him.

This is the ultimate danger of the Want-Assume-Misunderstand cycle — relationships that seem to fall apart out of nowhere. It's a huge relationship pitfall — one the rest of this book will help you avoid.

The Discovery Mind-Set

So how did we get this way? Have we always been poor at digging deeper and simply not been aware of it?

These are big questions with any number of possible answers. But I see a clear connection between our lack of investigative prowess and our ever-increasing technology mind-set. The amount of time we spend interacting with our devices *does* influence the way we learn to interact with each other, and, as we know, technology is teaching us some very unhelpful lessons.

As discussed earlier, the principle of efficiency is a big part of what we're learning from our devices. Now let's look at two more principles: data and discovery.

You may be surprised to learn that data and I are old friends. Before becoming a relationship coach, I was a performance marketer for various Silicon Valley start-ups. The "marketer" part of the job title is straightforward: I managed online and mobile advertising campaigns to get products seen by the public. The "performance" part of the job title is less obvious: it means I did this using data.

On my performance marketing team, all our decisions for determining "what the audience likes" were based on data. What the data said is what we did. This is because the data *knew things* about our audience that we could never know. It knew what you looked at, what you clicked on, what you purchased. It knew when you hesitated and when you finally decided to go for it. It knew what spurred that change of heart and what to do to reproduce it.

Over time, we performance marketers became very good at predicting what you — and people like you — are about. People who like purple are usually women. Women usually like word games. Women who like purple and word games tend to buy watches. It may sound silly, but these are the bits of knowledge — taken together to create a picture with ever-increasing clarity — that we use to shape your experience of your technology.

So what does this have to do with deeper conversations? Well, it has to do with *knowing*. Through data, we — the people creating your experience with your personal technology — get to know you. Instead of the old-fashioned ad man who imagines what customers want using his ingenuity and understanding of human psychology, the performance marketer knows what you want *because you tell her.*

Any time we perform an action on a connected device, we are telling that device — and its various partners and applications — who we are. We tell our devices who we are, and they change our experience to match. Data powerfully influences our experience of our personal technology in ways we don't fully grasp while we're using it.

Data is everywhere, from the ads you're shown while streaming a movie to the results you're shown for any given internet search. Data determines which flowers you're prompted to buy on Valentine's Day as well as which single people you meet on Match.com. It even lurks in our underwear drawers.

One company, the lingerie retailer AdoreMe, does rigorous testing in order to show its customers exactly what they want to see. According to an article published in *Fast Company* in 2014:

> AdoreMe subjects all of its images to testing every single month, going as far as to test one hand position against another, and in doing so has collected a trove of intel on what works and what doesn't. The photographer, a man, has some guidelines for what works in pictures: a certain distance between the camera and the model, a specific blurriness, particular positions that sell well. Hand on hip, a popular pose among Instagrammers trying to make their arms look skinny, doesn't resonate nearly as well as a hand on the head, for example. (That slight change can double sales, according to internal research.)

This data takeover matters because it's been instrumental in effecting a wide-sweeping change in how you interact with your technology. The whole online landscape is moving away from the idea that you, the user, should have to search for what you want online.

The internet of the very near future will be one of content discovery — what you want will simply appear before you. And not just what people *like you* want, but what *you* want. An article published on Forbes.com in 2014 describes this change in detail: "Over time the evolution of the Internet and advent of new platforms has fundamentally changed how we discover content.

Content discovery is no longer a simple query based on user input. Now, content discovery is automated, personalized, and much more contextual than ever before, and it's continually evolving. Content discovery is a process that helps you explore new topics or information without you having to search for them."

An article published on Inc.com in 2014 describes it similarly: "There is so much content on the Internet these days that it's often not helpful enough to do a search. Companies are now using [data] to know what you want ahead of time and bring it to you without any effort on your part."

Notice how these two quotes end: *"without you having to search for them"* and *"without any effort on your part."*

Here is how this all relates to what I see as our poorly developed investigative muscle. Our interactions with our personal technology are teaching us that we should not have to exert any effort to get the content we want. We should not have to dig, we should not have to search, we should not have to ask. The thing we're looking for — buried deep in a sea of information — should simply *appear.*

I believe these ways in which we're being taught to interact with our technology are affecting our mind-set about interactions *in general.* We are developing a discovery mind-set: "I should have to do as little as possible to get what I'm looking for" and "If you have something of value buried deep inside you, you better bring it to surface it on your own if you want me to know about it."

This is a fine way to think when the entity on the receiving end is the internet. But what if it's a person? Is this attitude really helping us to learn about one another? Or is it getting in the way?

I want to make clear that, if you're looking at the world through the discovery lens, it's really not your fault. Everyone develops habits and learns lessons from their environment, and there's no denying that technology is changing everyone's environment. It's not the technology's fault, either. Those who are pushing the data and discovery waves are simply trying to make personal technology more usable, more relevant, and more fun.

But if you want to get closer to other people, you will need to let go of the idea that deeper content should just surface on its own. You're going to have to "do a search," so to speak. You're going to have to make an effort. *Knowing* and *caring* are verbs, after all.

What does one actually *do* to start accessing this deeper content? To put it simply: start with wants, but don't stop with wants. It's the same lesson you picked up when learning to pick partners: start with attraction, but don't stop with attraction. Touch the surface and then begin digging. Ask questions, notice, investigate, and wonder.

Questions for Reflection

- What's one thing you may have assumed about someone that you'd like to have clarified?
- Have you ever been completely wrong about someone else's deeper intentions or motivations? How did that experience play out?
- Do you sense the discovery mind-set creeping into any of your relationships?

An Exercise to Challenge Yourself

Work to build awareness of your own curiosity. In any situation or interaction, ask yourself: "What am I curious about right now?" Make this a mantra you repeat to yourself throughout your day.

Chapter Summary

- The first step in creating closeness is mastering the art of knowing. The main challenge we face when it comes to knowing another person is that we typically focus on wants.

- While wants are not bad, they do mask a hidden meaning — the source of the want — which reveals much more about who the person is than the want itself. Remaining on the topic of wants indefinitely never lets us access this deeper source, or the deeper aspects of the person.

- Wants also breed assumptions. If you and I want the same thing, it's easy for me to assume that our wants spring from the same source, which very often is not the case. This can lead to great misunderstandings about each other's inner worlds.

- The technology mind-set plays a part in our fixation on wants. Personal technology is moving in the direction of giving the user exactly what he's looking for without his having to exert much (or any) effort. In other words, we are moving away from "search" and toward "discovery." The more we interact with our personal technology, the less trained we are to actively search.

- The way to discover these deeper aspects of another person is to investigate her wants. In other words, to search. Investigation is an activity — a skill — that you can learn.

Chapter 6

Drawing Deeper Understanding

It's time to start getting specific about how one gains deeper understanding of another person's inner world. As we learned in the last chapter, the place to start is with wants, and then we move beyond them. This chapter will show you how to propel the conversation past wants — and into discussing *what the wants mean.*

A want usually stems from a deeper source than the want itself. Often seemingly disparate wants can all be traced back to a single source. These sources of wants live within a person's core, in her heart and mind. Understanding them is the essence of understanding her.

So how do we start understanding these sources? First, we must understand what they are. The primary sources of wants are needs and values. People often use the words *needs* and *values* interchangeably, and there are indeed similarities between the two. The main similarity is that both needs and values are capable of answering the question "What do you care about?" A need represents something a person cares about. A value does the same.

Note that I'm using the word *care* in this definition of *needs* and *values.* As we know, caring is one of the two actions required to produce closeness. So what does it mean to care about something... that's not a person?

Let's look back at what it means to care about a person. Caring about a person entails feeling that her well-being matters to you and showing her that you care. These principles apply very naturally to caring about things as well — things such as ideas, principles, interests, missions, and goals.

Let's say, for example, that you care very deeply about equality; equality is one of your values. Equality is in and of itself an idea, a notion, a concept that exists outside you in much the same way another person does. You can have a particular relationship with the concept of equality, and another person can have a totally different relationship with it, in much the same way that it works with people. No two people have the exact same relationship with any given third person.

In other words, you can be in relationship with equality. But what does it mean to *care* about equality? Well, we know that the first part of caring about a person is to feel the feeling of caring: to feel the gravity — the *weight* — of caring about that person's well-being. You can indeed also care about equality's well-being. This would mean feeling in your heart that the concept of equality matters to you — that you want it to stay alive and well for as long as possible.

Caring about equality means wanting to be involved with it even when it's inconvenient to do so, even when other options offer more obvious benefits. A concept can take up space in one's heart in much the same way a person can.

But what about the second part of caring: showing someone you care? How could you show equality that you care? This may sound very strange indeed. Equality is a concept, an abstract. It doesn't need you to text it your condolences when it gets laid off. It doesn't need to cry on your shoulder when it's going through a breakup.

Well, no. But it does need your support when it's being

trampled on. It does need you to show up for it when you know it's in trouble. Demonstrating care for the well-being of a concept — *well-being* meaning its healthy presence in our society, institutions, and consciousness — is possible. It simply requires putting effort into helping the concept flourish.

Needs and values — the things we care about, the sources of our wants — matter because they are the contents of our core selves. They make up much of the terrain of our inner worlds.

Needs and Values

If needs and values can both answer the question "What do you care about?" then why are they considered separate notions? Why isn't there just one source of wants?

As I've said, needs and values are indeed highly interconnected. There will be times, in your process of gaining deeper understanding of another person, when it won't be important to distinguish whether you're exploring a need or a value. But there is an important distinction between the two: needs tend to be very similar for all people, whereas values tend to be highly individualized.

Another way to state this distinction is in the negative: when someone is not meeting one of her needs, she'll have a hard time functioning well — getting up in the morning, holding down a job, maintaining relationships. When a person is not honoring one of his values, he'll function fine by all outward assessments... but he will not *feel well* in his life.

Needs are the things that almost all people fundamentally require to function in life — but this doesn't mean we don't frequently deny or ignore them. Values, on the other hand, are the aspects of life that you choose to invest in to create your own special meaning. Needs are mostly chosen for us by the physical realities of our bodies; values, however, are chosen *by us*. Because of this difference, needs and values can be unearthed in different ways and then used in different ways to create closeness.

Needs

When most people hear the word *needs* they think of the basic physical necessities of life: air, water, food, shelter, protection from the elements. The most enduring framework for understanding needs is Maslow's hierarchy, which proceeds from physical necessities like food, water, and air, to safety and security, to love and belonging, to creativity and self-actualization.

This framework has endured for more than seventy years and is a nice place to start when pondering the role of needs. Because it's generally considered a one-size-fits-all model, it also reinforces the main difference between needs and values: that the same needs apply to everyone.

When I think about needs, I often think about a friend I made at one of my first performance marketing jobs. She was a highly creative designer, and one of the only other women at the company, so we became close quickly. We would commiserate about all the bros, the long hours, and all the energy drinks in the fridge. However, over time, much of the commiserating turned into all-out complaining. Her complaints — more often than not — centered on the long hours.

"The engineers don't even get in until noon! I've practically worked a whole day before they start. Then I'm expected to stay until they leave. It's exhausting," she grumbled.

"You could try coming in later, right?" I offered.

"I can't...I can never sleep in past seven!"

Even on Mondays, after the weekend had come and gone, she'd reiterate how exhausted she was.

"You didn't rest over the weekend?" I wondered.

"Can't! The weekend is the only time I have to see friends, do laundry, get groceries...I'm really wiped out."

In retrospect, I see now that this was fundamentally a needs problem. She was unable to meet one of the needs at the very bottom of Maslow's pyramid: rest. Many of our colleagues were denying some of their basic needs as well. Many didn't eat regular meals; some never seemed to leave their desks. In the end, those who behaved this way burned out — started functioning less and less well — much faster than the rest of us.

Some of the things that most of us require — our needs — are:

Safety
Protection from the elements
Respect
Autonomy
Self-determination
Freedom
Physical health
A functioning body
Having enough to eat
Sexual expression
Reliability
A predictable environment
Financial stability
Employment
Social ties
Social support
Excitement
Interests

As you probe deeper into another person's inner world, you'll often find she is not meeting some of her needs. Unmet needs tend to surface before disregarded values do, because when your body is craving something fundamental, it's hard to feel anything other than that unmet need. You can't eat before you can breathe; you can't build a shelter before you can eat; you can't think about your community before you can build a shelter; and you can't devote your life to equality before you can think about your community.

Values

Values, as opposed to needs, are highly individualized. One person's core value could sound like an absolute nightmare or a complete waste of time to someone else. This doesn't happen with needs. Two people would not get into a fight over whether it was a waste of time to care about obtaining clean drinking water.

So what exactly are values? Values are just what the word implies: things that have worth to you. Values can be as tangible as an antique writing desk that your grandfather entrusted to you. They can be as intangible as the concept of saving the earth. Values are anything — object, swath of land, idea, principle, mission, goal, relationship — that holds personal worth for you. You know it's a value if you feel compelled to invest your time and energy into it.

Many unfortunate things happen when we aren't aware that we have values or, for whatever reason, cannot make our values a priority. The most common result is a sinking feeling — a sense that our life is pointless or that life itself is worthless. Depression, malaise, melancholy...these are the hallmarks of a life without known and honored values. A life *with* known and honored values, on the other hand, feels like it has substantial personal worth and meaning.

There is an endless list of possible values, but some common ones are:

Learning
Humor
Artistry

Aesthetics
Achievement
Communing with nature
Altruism
Adventure
Nurturance
Exploration
Excellence
Mastery
Faith
Harmony
Honesty
Loyalty
Introspection
Leadership
Risk taking
Courage
Justice
Fairness
Resilience
Self-discipline
Responsibility
Style
Tradition

As I said, a defining characteristic of values is that they are highly personal and subjective. Even a very tangible value, such as an object, will not remain unchanged if transferred from one person to another. When your grandfather left you his antique writing desk, it took on great personal value to you. You know your grandfather loved this desk, and you want to keep it safe. But when you consider it, the desk had a different value to your grandfather than it does to you. He valued it for its usefulness.

You value it for sentimental reasons. And if you ever sold it to someone new, that person might value it simply for its beauty.

In other words, the desk itself is separate from the value each person places on it. This is the same for abstract values as well. Two people can value the notion of "elegance," but elegance will mean slightly (or very) different things to each of them, and they will honor the value of elegance in very different ways.

When it comes to needs, it's quite easy to see how unmet ones create wants. I have an unmet need for rest, so I want to sleep in or I want to go on vacation. With values, it's much more complex. A woman values elegance but is ignoring that fact, so...what would she want? Frankly, I have no idea.

The fact that I have no idea is important. It points to the fact that one person's value will not transfer unchanged to another person. This means that I really *can't* know what elegance means to her or what kinds of wants it would produce in her.

That is to say, I can't know unless I ask her.

Asking inviting questions — discussed at length in the next chapter — is absolutely essential for getting to know someone's deepest values. To truly see from another person's perspective, you have to see her *values* from her perspective. This is a challenge for everyone. But when we do it well — and we certainly can! — we will develop some of the deepest understanding possible with another person.

How to Identify Needs and Values

Needs and values show themselves in a variety of ways. Each has some characteristic patterns that make it possible to distinguish one from the other, even in casual conversation. At times your partner may identify and name his need or value as such without much investigation required on your part. But more often than not, he'll simply behave in certain, distinctive ways that point toward an unmet need or disregarded value.

The telltale signs of an unmet need are:

- Complaining
- Blaming and name calling
- Fearfulness, feeling threatened
- Gossiping (when in teams or groups)

My designer friend who consistently complained about being tired was expressing an unmet need in the form of complaining. Let's look at some other complaints that could contain an unmet need:

Presenting complaint: "My boss is micromanaging me."
Possible unmet need: freedom or self-determination

Presenting complaint: "My roommates are crazy."
Possible unmet need: personal space or a predictable environment

Presenting complaint: "I hate moving."
Possible unmet need: shelter or stability

Presenting complaint: "My friends are so flaky."
Possible unmet need: social support or predictability

Complaints are not necessarily a bad thing, as long as they don't persist or become damaging to the one who's complaining or to the relationship. An occasional complaint here and there is great — complaints can be incredibly useful. Being vocally upset about something is essentially pointing a finger right at it, saying, "I care about this!"

Use someone's complaints to your advantage in your pursuit

of deeper understanding. Instead of trying to diffuse the complaint or feed into it with your own (one of the biggest mistakes you can make in relating), use the energy of the complaint to go deeper. "You seem really upset about this situation. What about it is upsetting you?" The responses you will get are a part of her inner world.

A side note: identifying needs is a great place to start if you're stuck in the habit of making assumptions about people. It's much less problematic to assume another person needs food to be happy, just as you do, than it is to assume she values mastery of the trombone like you do.

It's less common for values to manifest as complaints. An unmet need — for food, water, rest, breathable air — produces an irritation, a drive to let others know you're not getting what you need. On the other hand, a disregarded value produces a malaise, an often vague sense of discontent. When people don't feel well but don't know how to articulate what's wrong, they tend to say nothing. The unmet need shouts for attention; the disregarded value slinks into the shadows.

The telltale signs of a disregarded value are:

- Withdrawal
- Disappointment
- Agitation or anxiety
- Frustration, the source of which remains vague

Let's look at some frustrations and how their source could be a disregarded value:

> **Presenting frustration:** "I like my job; I just don't feel like I'm learning anything anymore."
> **Possible disregarded value:** knowledge or personal growth

Presenting frustration: "I wish I could make more time to get out of the city."
Possible disregarded value: nature or serenity

Presenting frustration: "How come I'm so busy all the time but still feel like I'm not making progress?"
Possible disregarded value: balance or achievement

Presenting frustration: "After my kids go to sleep at night, I don't know what to do with myself."
Possible disregarded value: Really anything — you'd have to dig deeper!

If you're trying to be close to someone who's making statements of this sort, it's imperative that you explore the statements. This is what gaining access to another person's inner world is all about! When you can truly understand what these statements are about for the other person, you have gained profound knowledge of her.

The main challenge, of course, is that these statements can be slippery. The other person may herself have no idea why she feels a certain way. She may even resist putting her malaise into words because, frankly, it's uncomfortable. It makes most people feel vulnerable to start exposing what's behind their frustration or disappointment. But the details matter. Specificity creates closeness.

The difference between how needs and values present themselves solidified for me when I began coaching a young woman we'll call Madeline who was struggling with her parents. Her relationship with them had become strained because they didn't support her dream of becoming a documentary filmmaker. She had begun to emotionally withdraw from them.

To their credit, her parents agreed to come to coaching and, when they did, they described their perspective of the situation: they were giving her money every month and simply wanted her to get a "real job." They called her a spoiled brat and believed she needed to make her own living. "You feel not supported?" they scoffed. "We *literally* support you!"

As with all disputes among family members, this disagreement did not exist in isolation. Much had happened leading up to this point, and emotions were running high. But after some investigating, I came to understand that the conflict was fundamentally one of needs vs. values.

Madeline's parents were blaming her for being a "spoiled brat" — remember that name-calling is a telltale sign of an unmet need — and were clearly angry about her money situation. With a little digging, we uncovered that they were very fearful about their *own* money situation. In other words, their financial security was feeling threatened. They also wanted their daughter to be able to survive after they were gone — the fundamental need to ensure the survival of one's offspring.

Madeline, on the other hand, was focused on values. She felt her parents didn't understand that she was working toward something bigger — something that mattered to her more than making money. She dreamed of making documentary films because she wanted to give a voice to the voiceless. At her core, she wanted to promote honesty and transparency in the world. She was willing to sacrifice some of her needs for the time being in order to honor her core values.

The family eventually came to an agreement that suited them all. Madeline would get a flexible job that helped pay her bills and would work on her filmmaking the rest of the time. Her parents would save more of their own money and agreed to be more accepting of her career choice. But it was really the deeper understanding and acceptance of one another's needs and values that brought them closer.

Drawing Deeper Understanding, Drawing Closer

Learning about your partner's needs and values — the two sources of his or her wants — is a highly useful tool for creating closeness. Below are some guidelines to help you draw deeper understanding.

Recognize Needs

Because needs are often made vocal through complaining and so on, and usually have to be addressed before values, it's likely that when you start building closeness with someone through knowing him, you'll notice his needs right away. Any complaints, blaming of others for the situations in which he finds himself, or fearful language is usually an unmet need poking out its head. Simply notice these needs — it is not your job to resolve them — and work to understand how they are affecting his well-being.

Investigate Values

Values tend to require more exploring than needs do. Because they are so personal, an exploration of values between you and your partner tends to deepen the closeness between you. The effort you invest in putting words to values will help pull you together.

Remember, we don't typically talk about values in our everyday lives; we don't typically offer them up as topics of conversation. For these reasons, you will need to actively investigate values with your partner. Try not to fall back into the discovery mind-set — believing that the information should surface without any effort on your part. And try not to get frustrated when your partner doesn't know exactly what her feelings mean. This is a process.

One more note about values: it's not terribly important for you and your partner to share values. If this ends up becoming a serious relationship, it can be useful to have similar values down the road. But in general, try not to focus on how her values are like yours. This is a slippery slope that can lead toward making the conversation about you.

Instead, if a common value comes up, simply notice and remember it. That's an opportunity to create shared meaning and purpose down the road. If a common value never appears, you've still gained deeper understanding of the other person and garnered more closeness.

Retain What You've Learned

It isn't enough simply to learn about your partner's inner world. To build closeness, it's also crucial to retain the information you've learned, to integrate it into your image of the other person, and to treat him accordingly in the future. Remember the "ability to accept new information" required of any potential partner? This is the time for you to flex that muscle.

Retaining information about a potential partner is essential for intimacy. As social psychologist and relationship expert Susan E. Cross put it, "If individuals seek to develop and build a new relationship, they will not only respond sensitively and warmly when the relationship partner discloses to them, but they will also remember and act on this information."

In other words, *knowing* is an active verb.

Finally, allow your partner to change. Change is inevitable over a long-term relationship, so you might as well embrace it. If your partner loses interest in a particular value over time, that's perfectly natural. Simply make sure to keep your picture of his inner world up-to-date, and treat him accordingly going forward. Changes are moments to reinvestigate and redraw the picture.

Questions for Reflection

- Have you noticed yourself or your partner regularly complaining about things? What needs might be going unmet?
- Have you noticed yourself or your partner acting withdrawn? What values might need to come to the surface?
- Are differences of needs and values causing any conflicts in your life right now (as they were for Madeline and her parents)? How might approaching the conflict from a needs-vs.-values perspective help?

 ## An Exercise to Challenge Yourself

Review the lists of needs and values in this chapter. Which stick out to you? Pick ten that strike you as important, and journal about what each one means to you.

Chapter Summary

- Our wants have two sources: needs and values. They both produce wants because they are capable of answering the question "What do you care about?" Understanding what another person needs and values gives you much deeper access to her inner world.
- The difference between needs and values is that needs tend to be very similar for all people, whereas values tend to be highly personal. Needs are the things that almost all

people require to function well in their lives. Values are the things each person requires to *feel well* in her life.

- How do we distinguish a need from a value? Unmet needs tend to call attention to themselves loudly — through complaining or blaming. Disregarded values tend to be quieter. They usually produce a sense of malaise or frustration that's hard to pin down.

- Remember, you're not learning about your partner's needs so you can *do* anything about them; you're not trying to change or influence them. You're simply trying to gain a deeper understanding of the other person, achieve deeper knowing, create more closeness, and reduce your loneliness.

Chapter 7

Asking Inviting Questions

We all know from experience that asking questions is a great way to get to know another person. Many of us, however, underestimate the true importance of question asking in conversation. Maybe we are intimidated by questions; maybe we don't want to be intrusive. Either way, question asking will still need to become a go-to tool in your knowing toolkit.

Questions matter for many reasons. First and foremost, they keep our conversations from becoming coordinated monologues — conversations in which I'm focused on talking about me and you're focused on talking about you. These types of interactions leave little room for crossing the boundary between you and me — to gain direct access to each other. These are the interactions from which you'll walk away feeling lonelier than before you came, often without fully understanding why.

Questions cross the divide between "my story" and "your story" because the process of asking and answering them brings both people into the recounting of a story. Both people become part of a story; both people become involved.

I would venture to say that questions are *the* conversational skill needed for helping us know one another. They encourage the other person to share more details of her inner world than she normally would. And, just as important, questions demonstrate interest in the other person. Demonstrating interest is a vital form of caring, one that you will learn about more in later chapters. For now suffice it to say that questions are one of the best ways to communicate that you've noticed and care about what your partner is saying.

To get a sense of the importance of questions, let's look at an article published on the *New York Times* website titled "To Fall in Love with Anyone, Do This." The article, written by Mandy Len Catron, details the experience of testing out psychologist Arthur Aron's famous social experiment in which he succeeded at making two people fall in love in his lab. How did he do it? By having them ask each other thirty-six questions... and afterward stare into each other's eyes for four minutes. The list of thirty-six questions included:

- If you could change anything about the way you were raised, what would it be?
- Is there something that you've dreamed of doing for a long time? Why haven't you done it?
- If you knew that in one year you would die suddenly, would you change anything about the way you are now living?
- If you were going to become a close friend with your partner, please share what would be important for him or her to know.

In the article — which went absolutely viral — Catron confesses that she tried out the questions and later the eye gazing with a man she barely knew, a "university acquaintance." Did she and the acquaintance fall in love after the experiment? They did! Of course, Catron knew in her heart — and said as much — that she was attracted to this guy-about-campus before they embarked on the experiment. It's likely they picked each other to experiment on because they kinda liked each other already. Did the questions really *cause* love? I don't think we can know.

But I love this story because it's about closeness. Two people felt attracted to each other, got to know each other through the active effort of knowing — specifically, question asking — and became close very quickly. As Catron herself put it: "I see now that the story isn't about us; it's about what it means to bother to know someone, which is really a story about what it means to be known."

Purposeful intimacy can happen, and questions help make it possible. Questions unveil certain truths — certain internal realities — that don't frequently come to the surface unless drawn out by a question. Questions shine a light on the dimly lit places in one's inner world.

That's exactly what we're doing here, right? So let's learn how to craft the types of questions that allow us to know someone and be known in return. There are many more than thirty-six!

Why Questions Work

Before diving in to crafting your own excellent questions for accelerated knowing, let's take a moment to understand why questions are so powerful in this context. We mentioned a few reasons earlier: they allow you both to be included in the telling of your stories, they give your partner an opportunity to say more about her inner world, and they demonstrate interest in the other person, which is a form of caring.

The final reason that questions matter is something I think very few of us ever think about: our language is quite limited when it comes to describing subjective experiences. Language is a challenging hurdle when you're trying to know someone else's inner world — a place that's completely subjective. Questions unearth more of the nuances of subjective experience, allowing the total experience to be better understood.

Let me give you an example. Once when I was a child, I burned my finger on a lightbulb. If I were to tell you the story of this event, it would likely go no further than that — I burned my finger on a lightbulb. Would you get the sensation of what that experience was like for me from that one statement? Probably not. But if you asked me some questions, you could *feel* the experience for yourself. Did it sting? Did it leave a scar? Were you scared of lightbulbs after that? A few simple questions will help you form a much richer understanding of another person's subjective experiences.

To better understand why language is a hurdle, let's look back briefly on how and why human language arose. We don't know exactly how old spoken language is, but we know that our ancestors first started using sounds to communicate information. It can be argued that usefulness — in the most practical sense of that word — is the fundamental purpose of language. If language had a mission statement, it would be: I'm a utilitarian tool for conveying objective information about the world.

In ancient times a word like *flower* would mean the same thing to every person in the same tribe. *Flower* would relate to the same construct in everyone's mind — that was the point of giving it a word. "Go pick a flower" would be the same command, no matter who you said it to.

If there were a reason to make a new distinction, the tribe would develop two separate words. If the tribe members learned that one flower — "oleander" — was poisonous and another flower — "rose" — was medicinal, they would develop a separate word for each. Everyone would understand why these two were distinct and required their own words, and the universal understanding of what each word represented would continue.

This evolution of language is astonishingly effective — really one of the greatest of human accomplishments — when you're trying to convey *objective information*. The issue is that when you're speaking about subjective information, this chain of words-and-meaning does not survive unbroken. When I say "rose," you probably know what I mean. But when I say "authenticity," do you know what I mean? When I say "freedom," do you know what I mean? Do you *really* know what I mean?

Language is no longer just for conveying objective information. It's no longer simply for getting something done safely and correctly. It's also for conveying information about one's experiences…one's feelings, memories, sensations, dreams, and desires. These take much more active investigation, and many more words, to communicate well.

There is absolutely an art to the finely crafted question. It must strike a balance between being "too soft" and "too hard." Questions that are too soft — too vague or meek — produce flimsy or not fully formed responses. Questions that are too hard — too jarring or accusatory — produce resistance and defensiveness in your partner. How does one go about achieving a balance? And how does one maintain this balance in a real back-and-forth conversation?

I'll address the second question first. While there may be an art to the finely crafted question, there is no script. To come up with good questions in the moment, the key is maintaining an inviting mind-set. In other words, think of questions as invitations.

Imagine that asking a friend a question is like mailing him a wedding invitation. Sending someone a wedding invitation does not mean that person is required to show up. He may not be able to, for good reasons. If he can't, you'll likely feel disappointed, but it (I hope) doesn't mean you'll never invite him to anything ever again. On the receiving end, getting a wedding invitation in the mail feels exciting — it's so nice that she cares enough to invite you! You will definitely go if you can.

This is very similar to the giving and receiving of questions. The mind-set when you ask a question should be "I would love it if you could tell me more about this particular thing, but if you can't, I understand." What you'll find is that the more inviting you make the question, the more likely it is that the other person will "show up" and answer it.

On the receiving end, the person being asked the question should feel as if she's been handed a thoughtful invitation — an opportunity — to do something special with you. Sharing your inner world with another is extraordinary. It *is* a special occasion. Treat it that way!

Maintaining an inviting mind-set, especially when you're first getting to know someone, will rapidly deepen and broaden the self-disclosures between you two. Now let's return to the first question: How does one go about crafting a balanced question — one that's not too hard and not too soft?

Why "Why" Doesn't Work

One hallmark of a too-hard question is that it doesn't elicit an answer that's any more expansive than what someone would have told you without being asked. In fact, the person may even end up telling you *less*. Too-hard questions don't work well because they prime the other person to retreat, shutting down the conversation. And as we know, there's no knowing without conversation.

So what makes a question too hard? It can be an accusatory tone, or a certain phrasing that belies judgment. The question may criticize the other person, such as "What kind of idiot do you have to be...?" It may be recriminating, such as "How could you do that?!" Most of us pick up the underlying implications when we hear these kinds of questions.

At times, hard questions spring up innocently from a desire to seem smart. "Wouldn't it be better to...?" is a question that may seem smart and right, but it's still too hard because it incites your partner to retreat.

One type of too-hard question is so pervasive in our everyday language that it deserves its own discussion: the "why" question. The single fastest way to put someone on the defensive and make him feel interrogated is to ask a question that starts with "Why?" Why is that?

The "why" question doesn't work for creating closeness because it prompts the other person to defend her actions. This is the essence of defensiveness and the enemy of deeper understanding. Let's take a hypothetical situation to illustrate this point.

Imagine a young man brings his girlfriend home to meet his mom. After chatting and having dinner, the mom asks her son what she believes is an innocuous question: "Why do you like her?"

The son immediately bristles. What do you think would be his most likely responses? Sarcastic: "I don't know, why do you like dad?" Accusatory: "You mean you don't like her?" Straight-up defensive: "I like her because I like her!"

Instead, imagine she had asked the same question, rephrased: "What do you like about her?" Do you feel the difference?

The question "What do you like about her?" compels the son to think about what he likes in his girlfriend. He reflects for a second. He likes the way she carries herself. He likes that she's ambitious and funny. Yes, that's what he likes about her. Because of this small shift in wording, he and his mother have both learned something about what he likes in a partner.

The redeeming quality of the "why" question is that it can almost always be transformed into a "what" or "how" question. "What" and "how" questions evoke self-reflection, specificity…a deeper look at one's own inner world.

Resist the idea that these small changes in language make no difference. Asking "why" makes the askee want to justify her actions. A small change in wording can help her reflect, consider, and find evidence that either supports or challenges her actions.

The next time you sit down to eat dinner or watch a movie ask yourself, "Why am I doing this?" Feel the anxiety this question provokes: "Should I be doing something else? If I'm questioning it, I'm probably doing something wrong!" This is exactly the feeling that too-hard questions evoke. And it's exactly the feeling you want to avoid when getting to know your partner.

The Well-Crafted Question

Questions must have some firmness to them, or what's the point of asking them? A too-soft question — one that does not encourage your partner to think or feel any deeper — doesn't work, either.

Let's revisit the two friends who were both interested in buying homes. We know that interaction was an opportunity for them to understand each other's deeper motivations better and to grow closer. If they asked each other only too-soft questions such as "How many square feet are you looking for?" or "How many bedrooms do you want?" this would not be a conversation from which they'd walk away feeling closer. They'd know more about their theoretical houses but not more about each other.

You'll recognize that you're asking too-soft questions when the conversation starts to dwell on trivialities. In general, this is not as damaging to the relationship as the defensiveness provoked by a too-hard question, but it's not terribly helpful, either. Too-soft questions don't create distance…they just don't move you any closer.

So with your inviting mind-set activated, your goal is to create a balanced question. *Balance* means not too hard and not too soft, but it also (in this context) means *simple*. Think of it like this: it's much harder to balance many objects on a tightrope than it is to balance just one. Questions get clumsier the more you tack on to them, and they run the risk of landing either too hard or too soft. Simplicity is key.

So how does one craft a simple, balanced, thought-provoking question? It's easier than you think.

The first step is just to notice: Which aspects of what my partner is saying am I curious about? What do I sense he's leaving out? Notice any wants, complaints (needs), or areas where he seems withdrawn (values). These are your question topics.

While you're learning the art of question asking, it's perfectly fine to ask the question you really want to ask in your head, no matter how hard or soft it is. I do this all the time. The key is to quickly transform the question into an inviting one before giving voice to it. With a little practice, you'll get so fast at doing this, the delay will be unnoticeable.

To transform your question, first remove any accusatory language. Turn it into a "what" or "how" question if it was going to be a "why" question. Important words to notice in your original question are *don't, can't, should,* or *shouldn't*. These belie judgments that the other person may pick up on.

Then state your question in as few words as possible. Shorter questions are better because they strike a better balance between hard and soft (think of the tightrope). Asking shorter questions also makes it easier for you to leave yourself out of the question.

In the pursuit of sounding smart in front of other people,

many of us are conditioned to ask questions that contain some of the answers we expect to hear. This is very common in business settings, where we want to ask questions to demonstrate interest but also want to show we already know the answers. An example of this might be: "Don't you think it would improve sales to do TV ads?" as opposed to "What you do think could improve sales?"

This is perhaps a fine habit for business meetings, but it doesn't work well when you're trying to build closeness. Inserting an assumed answer in the question doesn't gain you any deeper access to another person's inner world.

Let's imagine our partner is unhappy because his boss isn't showing him enough respect. Here are some ways you might respond that are far "too smart":

1. Why do you think your boss can't respect you?
2. What's the problem with her wanting to check up on you?
3. What should you be doing differently?

Do you hear all the assumptions being made? Let's try to distill them:

In the first question, "Why do you think your boss can't respect you?" I hear an assumption that his boss *can't* respect him, which you don't know for sure and is unlikely true. In the second, "What's the problem with her wanting to check up on you?" I hear a value judgment; this question implies that I think the boss's behavior is probably right and that my partner's behavior is probably wrong. In the third, "What should you be doing differently?" I am implying that I think my partner *should* be doing something differently. As polite as this question appears to be, it's actually assigning blame.

Let's transform these questions. For the sake of simplicity, we'll keep our transformed versions to six words or less:

- What's important about that?
- How do you feel about that?
- What could change that?
- What might be causing that?
- How would that look?
- What else?

What's your first reaction to these questions? If it's that they're dumb, you're not alone! These types of questions sounded dumb to me too when I first started asking them. But the thing is, they *work*. They are, in fact, not dumb at all; rather, they are *spacious*. They allow for any response that naturally arises in another. They hold no bias, no implications, no assumptions, and no answers. They simply communicate: "I'm here with you. What would you like to say?"

To recap the steps for forming a balanced, inviting question in the moment:

1. Notice! What are you curious about? What wants, complaints, or areas of low energy do you hear?
2. Ask the question in your head the way you would normally ask it.
3. Remove "whys," assumptions, and leading or accusatory language.
4. Say the question out loud in as few words as you possibly can. Shoot for six words or less.
5. Notice what's in your partner's answer, return to step 1, and repeat!

If, in the moment, you're struggling to think of a balanced, inviting question, try my favorite catchall question: "What does that get you?" This is a great knowing question because it's spacious enough to accommodate any answer (not too hard or too smart) but encourages the other person to reflect on how her thoughts and actions are serving her.

I first read about the classic negotiation scenario, described below, in Roger Fisher's *Getting to Yes*. It's a perfect situation in which asking the question "What does that get you?" would make all the difference:

Two people are arguing over a lemon. There's only one lemon left, and they both want it. A negotiator comes in and convinces them that the only fair solution is to cut the lemon in half and give half to each. Neither party is satisfied with that solution, but they agree it's the only choice.

After the lemon is cut, the first person takes her half, squeezes the lemon juice into her water, and throws the rest away. The second person takes her half, throws away the fruit, and uses the peel to make a lemon cake.

What makes this an epic negotiation fail? Both parties could have had *all* of what they wanted if the negotiator had asked each, "What does the lemon get you?" For one, a lovely beverage; for the other, a cake. Never forget — even in the simplest of situations — that wants rarely tell the whole story.

Comprehending Answers

As you know, one question does not a conversation make. So how does one create a true, flowing conversation out of questions?

As my model for question asking above implies, more questions will come out of your first inviting question. You may cycle through the five steps listed above many, many times before landing on something that's significant to the other person. But eventually, you *will* land on something that matters — something that's vital to understanding her inner world. What happens then?

At that point, your goal switches from asking well-crafted questions to comprehending what is being said...*really* comprehending what's being said. This involves listening — *really* listening — to what is being said, interpreting it, and then checking your interpretation with your partner. If she likes your interpretation, internalize it and remember it.

Once your interpretation has been confirmed and you've solidified it in your own internal world, now you have a direct link between your two inner worlds.

Some well-established techniques for listening and then checking your interpretation will help you in this process:

- **Restating.** Restating is essentially repeating back exactly what your partner said. This is less about interpreting and more about making sure you are really hearing him accurately (and not missing anything important). Restating is valuable because it allows your partner to hear himself and amend his statements if he wants to.

- **Reframing.** Reframing is putting her thoughts — if she's expressing them in narrow and divisive terms — into more open and inclusive terms. Reframing is less about changing the meaning of her words and more about interpreting them in a way that allows them to fit into a larger, more useful framework.

- **Reflecting.** Reflecting is telling your partner what you're noticing. It's like holding up a mirror to him. This can be as simple as telling him you notice that his foot shakes like crazy when he talks about his girlfriend. The value of reflecting is that your partner is giving off lots of information while he is speaking and thinking about what to say. This information is usually missed entirely because it's not what he's focused on. Reflecting gives the information back to him.

- **Summarizing.** Summarizing is pulling together important ideas to produce overarching themes in what your partner is saying. The value of summarizing is that it helps her make connections between seemingly dissimilar ideas and allows her to let go of ideas that don't connect to the larger themes.

- **Validating.** Validating is simply expressing that you understand and can relate to what your partner is saying. Validating is valuable because deep conversations often lead to places where your partner will feel unsure if he's making sense or being reasonable. These conversations tend to go into uncharted territory, and validating lets your partner know that he's safe and cared for.

As you're practicing these skills, allow your conversation partner to correct or amend your interpretation of what she's said. A correction is absolutely not a failure! This is the process everyone goes through to accurately understand another person's inner world.

In addition to allowing for corrections, watch how your interpretation affects her. A shrug, a sigh, a nod, a quizzical head tilt...these all hold information about whether or not you've got it right. Fundamentally, you're looking for resonance, evidence that your partner has connected emotionally to your interpretation of her inner experience. When you have resonance, you have knowing.

Let's pull it all together:

You meet up with your friend Zak. Zak starts talking about how his boss micromanages him and how he's fed up with it. You notice that Zak is complaining — that probably means there's a need somewhere that's not being met. Get curious about what it is.

Your first inviting question could be: "How does that make you feel?"

Zak's response: "It makes me feel like she doesn't respect me."

This is good information. He's identified the unmet need

as respect. Now's the moment to resist the urge to assume you already know what respect means to Zak. You don't...yet. You only know what respect means to *you.*

Follow-up inviting question: "What would respect look like?"

Zak's response: "She would get off my back and let *me* make the important decisions about my project."

This is fun, right? Now it's time to check in and make sure that your interpretation of his response is correct. Allow him to correct your interpretation if he wants. Pick one of your checking-in techniques, and go!

Reframing: "So respect would include giving you space and trusting your judgment?"

Zak's response: "That's right!"

Do you see how you could go really deep with this? "How much space would be enough space?" "How would it feel to know she trusts your judgment?" "How would that change your experience of being at work?" *These* are the conversations from which people walk away feeling closer.

A Note about Technology and Questions

Before we leave this topic, I want to issue one word of caution regarding questions: questions and technology do not always mix. For the purposes of building closeness, the medium through which you ask questions is very important. Technology can ruin a perfectly good question.

In the same way that language matters, the mode of communication matters as well. The best mode for investigating our inner world is the one that includes the most layers of communication. If it's between using email and the phone, use the phone, because it adds back in voice tone. If it's between the phone and a video chat, use a video chat because it adds back in visual cues such as facial expressions and body language. If it's between a video chat and talking in person, always go in person.

Having as many layers of communication as possible aids the process because the types of questions you'll be asking, such as "What does that get you?" or "What's important about that?" evoke all different kinds of responses. Some of the responses will be nonverbal. A long pause after a certain question has meaning that can be picked up face-to-face but not over email. An eye roll after a certain question has meaning that can be picked up face-to-face but not over the phone. You're very likely missing information when you don't have every layer of communication available to you.

Another problem with asking inviting questions online or over a text is that it ruins silences. Silences are one of the most powerful ways to allow someone to reflect, to take it in, to process, and to respond to your questions thoughtfully. Over email, phone, and often even video chat, silence is perceived as dead air. This is one of the best investigative tools you have, reduced to nothing more than awkwardness.

Last, when you're choosing when/where/how/with what mode of communication to explore another person's inner world, be extremely careful about whether the communication is public or private. A balanced and inviting question such as "How's the roommate situation going?" has a totally different subtext if it's written on your brother's Facebook wall vs. being sent as a private message. He'll know you *could have* sent the message privately and chose not to.

Public questioning in this fashion runs the risk of putting the other person on the spot. If you're asking something that could potentially sound too hard, it instantly will. Even if you're asking something caring and kind, the fact that you posted it publicly can taint even the most heartfelt message.

Take a question like "How are you adjusting to the new baby?" Communicated privately, it simply conveys that you'd like to know how your friend's adjusting to the new baby. Communicated publicly, it says something more like "I'd like to know how you're adjusting to the new baby...and I'd like everyone to know I'm nice enough to ask." Unfortunately, the public nature of the message makes it seem as if you want credit for caring.

Possibly even worse, the above question could imply, "I'm concerned you're *not* adjusting well to the baby, and others should be concerned too." This subtext would be a really unfortunate outcome of a perfectly well-meaning question. Of course, negative subtext won't always be the consequence of public questioning, but it is a possibility to be cautious of.

Questions for Reflection

- How do you typically ask questions when getting to know someone? Do your questions usually fall on the side of too hard or too soft?
- What's your natural style of deeper exploration? Are you more apt to notice subtle emotions flicker across a face? Or are you more attuned to what's not being said?
- Have you ever questioned someone publicly, then realized you probably should have done it privately? What were the repercussions?

 An Exercise to Challenge Yourself

Pick a day when you are around people, and don't utter any sentence that's longer than six words at a time. This will teach you economy of language and the beauty of saying less.

Chapter Summary

- Questions matter in your efforts to get to know someone; the specific language you use to ask a question matters too. The same question asked two different ways will yield two different answers. Much of the language we use in everyday life is not equipped for talking about highly subjective matters, like a person's inner world, so asking good questions can be a challenge.

- You can get around the limitations of language by maintaining an inviting mind-set. You are not coaxing, probing, or interrogating your partner with your questions; each question is simply an invitation to share.

- Attempt to balance your questions between being too soft and too hard. Questions that are too soft — too vague or shallow — produce flimsy or not fully formed responses. Questions that are too hard — too jarring or accusatory — produce resistance and tend to shut down conversation.

- The steps for forming a balanced, inviting question are:

  1. Notice! What are you curious about?
  2. Ask the question in your head the way you would normally ask it.
  3. Remove "whys," assumptions, and leading or accusatory language.
  4. Ask the question using as few words as possible.
  5. Notice what's in your partner's answer, return to step 1, and repeat!

- Last, be careful of the medium through which you ask questions. Asking via a device can turn a perfectly well-crafted question into one latent with subtext.

Chapter 8

Listening to Another Person's Narrative

The last three chapters served as your guide to mastering the art of knowing someone in the present moment. So far, you've learned how to acknowledge wants, dig deeper, understand what your partner really cares about, and continue the cycle of learning about her through finely crafted questions. These skills are relevant at any stage in a relationship and can be applied to pretty much any conversation to create truer and deeper knowing.

But there's still an essential skill set we need to acquire in our quest of knowing someone fully. These are the skills of knowing someone in time — knowing about her past and her future. This aspect of knowing is critical for creating closeness because our memories of the past and visions of the future are at the heart of how we view the present moment.

Knowing Each Other in Time

In the most practical sense, knowing how to talk to someone about her past and future is valuable simply because these conversations inevitably come up when you hang out with someone more than once or twice. In fact, for some people, these are the default topics of conversation. So we need to know what to do when these topics arise.

On a deeper level, knowing someone in time matters for closeness because the past and future do not stand in isolation from the present. For most of us, our past and future selves are always with us.

You likely have direct knowledge of how your past lives within you. Perhaps you almost drowned when you were a child, and that event lives in you as a fear of deep water, or as a fascination with underwater life, or as a recurring nightmare. Many of your thought patterns, reactions to situations, habits, fears, and desires will spring directly from past experiences. The same is true of your partner.

While we don't always consciously know how our past experiences shape our life, sometimes we do. The ones that live in the forefront of our minds tend to be lessons. Perhaps your partner got married and divorced at a young age, and that experience now lives in him as this lesson: "Don't take commitments lightly. Don't give your word unless you mean it."

These lessons-from-memory can be the most influential lessons we ever learn, since we've experienced the pain of not following them. There is even evidence that the things we learn from memory have more direct control over our in-the-moment choices than anything that's happening in the moment. In her hugely popular book *All Joy and No Fun*, Jennifer Senior touches on this phenomenon while recounting her conversation with a young father named Paul:

> "But here's the thing," says Paul. "I would bet that if someone did a study and asked, 'Okay, your kid's three, rank these aspects of your life in terms of enjoyment,' and then, five years later, asked, 'Tell me what your life was

like when your kid was three,' you'd have totally different responses." With this simple observation, Paul has stumbled onto one of the biggest paradoxes in the research on human affect: we enshrine things in memory very differently from how we experience them in real time. The psychologist Daniel Kahneman has coined a couple of terms to make the distinction. He talks about the "experiencing self" versus the "remembering self." The experiencing self is the self who moves through the world and should therefore, at least in theory, be more likely to control our daily life choices. But that's not how it works out. Rather, it is the remembering self who plays a far more influential role in our lives, particularly when we make decisions or plan for the future.

In other words, to know someone's *whole self*, you'll need to get to know her experiencing self *and* her remembering self.

The ways in which the future lives in us today are a bit more abstract. The future tends to show itself as motivation to do things we don't always want to do in order to make a greater gain later. It lives in us as resilience, a sense of hope. We may act against our experiencing self's interests — forcing ourselves to go to the gym even though we'd rather not, for example — for the benefit of our future selves. The actions we take now to achieve some future goal show how the future, though just an idea, very much resides in us right now.

Listening to and honoring the stories that another carries about her past and future is absolutely fundamental to understanding her as a whole person. These stories are at the core of her inner world. It might not be a stretch to say that they are the land on which all her inner life grows.

The mental construct that each of us fosters — the idea of "myself through time" — is incredibly powerful. It influences how we organize our experiences. Understanding time linearly, as most people do, creates the mental construct of "My Story": the narrative I tell myself about where I came from and where I'm going.

One of the most impactful aspects of the My Story construct is that it gives us the ability to look back on something painful and infuse it with meaning and purpose. A devastating loss helped you grow stronger. "I became a better person because that happened." "I wouldn't be who I am today if I hadn't gone through that." "Everything happens for a reason." This is how we transform memories into meaning. This is how we make memories *useful* to our present selves.

The past provides context and reasons for where we are now. We can compare our present selves to our past ones to see how (and in what ways) we've grown. Because of this, knowing your partner in the past helps you know him better now; knowing him in the future also helps you know him better now.

The future is where your partner's potential lies. When he thinks about the future, that's when he has access to his image of his higher self — his better self. This envisioned better self reveals many of his deepest needs and values. If he says, "I want to have climbed Mount Everest by the time I'm forty," that almost certainly means that he values adventure and achievement. It wouldn't occur to him to go after that goal in the future if he didn't value those things in the present.

So how does one go about listening to another person's narrative in a way that fosters closeness?

How to Discuss the Future

The main challenge I've found with discussing the future is that most people interpret "discussing the future" as "planning for the future." This is *not* your goal when you're trying to get close. You're not trying to get your partner to prepare for or to commit to doing anything in particular. Your goal is simply to understand her inner world; resist the urge to try to *do* anything about it.

To keep discussions about the future from sliding into planning mode, it's best to hold tight to your inviting mind-set. Stay curious but loose. "What would you like to have happen down the road? What would you like to be different? What might that look like?" To keep the conversation loose, it's vital to ask open-ended questions, ones that can't be answered with a simple yes or no. They are great for talking about the future because they tend to evoke more expansive answers than short-sighted ones.

In conversations about the future (and about the past, for that matter), you can be less careful about the language you use when posing questions. It's unlikely that what your partner is telling you is new information to her (as opposed to when she talks about her needs and values, which very well may be new information to her). You're much less likely to make your partner defensive discussing these topics, and you're much less likely to derail her from a story that's deeply ingrained in her memory with a slightly leading question.

The open-ended questions you ask when discussing the future can be more directive — the goal is simply to demonstrate interest. You can ask about a specific time or place in the future or about a specific aspect of the future:

- What do you want to be doing ten years from now?
- Where would be the perfect place to live for you? What would it look like?
- If you had all the money you wanted, what would you do with it?

The content of your partner's responses is worth noting and remembering, but it's not really the main focus here. The narrative itself is less important than *how the narrative is told*. Listen to what is being said and *how* it's being said. Like other types of self-disclosures, the factual content is valuable, but the emotional content is priceless.

Notice: Does she describe the future with excitement? Does she worry about repeating past mistakes in the future? Is she angry about acquiring more and more responsibility as she grows up? It's the tone and feeling of these discussions that reveal far-reaching moods (positive, negative, triumphant, confused) about her life.

It's also vital to listen to what is not being said. If, when you two were growing up, your cousin always talked about having kids and yet conspicuously leaves that out of her ten-year vision, there's something to that. Maybe she's changing her mind and doesn't know how to talk about it. This is information; this is her inner world.

I also recommend listening for themes in your partner's description of the future. This is a story, after all! What's a story without themes? If you listen, you'll hear that some aspects of the future are more at the forefront of her mind than others. For one person, everything you ask her may come back around to work. For another, everything may relate to travel. For others, family is everything. Notice these trends, and use your summarizing skills.

These themes — these trends — usually reveal themselves naturally throughout the course of getting to know someone. But if for some reason they don't — because your partner is consistently being vague — I recommend asking her to weigh her responses. In other words, ask: How much weight does this vision of the future hold for you vs. that one? On a scale of 1 to 10, how important is it for you to live in another country someday? For you to have kids? For you to lead a spiritual life? While this might sound rather cold and clinical, taking something as abstract as a vision of the future out of the qualitative realm and putting it into the quantitative helps firm it up.

Last, notice how some of the things your partner describes about her future are really expectations — things she strongly *believes* will happen — and some are dreams — things she very much *hopes* will happen. Touching on both of these gives you the most complete understanding of how she sees her future.

Expectations and dreams play out differently and lead to different consequences. Expectations tend to feel within reach, so if they end up being unmet in the future, your partner will experience this as very disappointing — possibly even devastating. On the other hand, dreams tend to feel like stretches, so if they don't pan out in the future, she'll be more likely to accept that it didn't work out and move on.

But dreams have power that expectations don't. Dreams are what motivate us to do better, to *be* better. A dream can be the compass by which you chart the course of your whole life, whereas most expectations go wholly unnoticed. Both matter, but in the end, dreams are what make people come alive.

Tips for talking about the future:

- Maintain an inviting mind-set.
- Ask open-ended questions.
- Listen to what your partner says…and *how* she says it.
- Notice what is not being said.
- Identify themes.
- Differentiate between expectations and dreams.

How to Discuss the Past

Discussing the past tends to be more challenging than discussing the future for a number of reasons. The first is that the future is full of possibilities, and most people — if they're in a decent frame of mind about their life — can imagine a brighter future. The past, however, is written in stone. It cannot be changed, and most of the opportunities it offers are opportunities to learn and grow. But as we as know, learning and growing can be painful.

The past — memories specifically — are also inextricably tied to emotions, which we'll discuss more in the next chapter. There's really no way to discuss the past in any detail without stirring up emotions. It can be difficult to see your partner experiencing strong emotions, but don't let a few tears deter you! Many people consider conversations about the past (about childhood, specifically) to be the most intimate discussions possible.

Getting to know about your partner's past is also incredibly useful. Since his past experiences play an enormous role in shaping his perspective, knowing how that perspective came to be helps you see from it as well. In other words, if you know how the lens through which your partner sees the world was formed, you can more easily see through that lens as well.

That lens can certainly change with time, but for most of us, our early life experiences form at least part of the filter through which we see the world, even in our adult lives. This filter affects how we interpret things today. Understanding your partner's filter allows you to fairly accurately predict how she'll perceive life events as they're happening. This type of prediction — the type rooted in seeing through the other person's lens — is not about making assumptions. It is true knowing in action.

So how do you approach talking about the past?

First, engage in the stories your partner tells about his past when they arise naturally in conversation, because they usually will. When he opens the door to the past, get curious. Demonstrate interest. He may be unsure whether you really want to hear about things that aren't directly relevant to you, so be encouraging, and maintain an inviting mind-set.

I want to note here that you're trying to learn more about his perspective, not trying to figure out the ways in which his childhood was similar or dissimilar to your childhood. Try not to let every statement about his parents trigger your feelings about your parents. If a similarity arises, it's perfectly fine to mention it, but make an effort not to reroute the conversation to being about you.

To maintain interest and avoid getting too involved in thinking about your own past, it can help to think about your partner's story as if it were a novel or a movie. If you were watching an interesting movie, what kinds of questions would naturally arise?

- Who are the characters?
- What is the setting like?
- Who is in conflict with whom?
- What are the characters' motivations?
- What are they learning from their mistakes?
- What are the characters acting oddly about, and why?

Again, notice *how* your partner tells the story. What's the mood of the story? If it were a movie, would it be in black and white or in vibrant color? Would it be told in a linear fashion or would it jump around in time? Would it be triumphant — with him overcoming many challenges? Is it a real tearjerker?

Becoming engaged when stories naturally arise is the easiest and most common way to learn about someone's past. But there are two situations in which you'll have to do more than that. The first is when your partner is telling the same story over and over again; the second is when she never tells a story about her past at all.

If your partner tells you the same story regularly with little variation, it may well be a sign that she's conveying an important episode in her life that she has not fully processed. People rarely recount the same event repeatedly unless there's something underneath the story.

121

This situation is not that far from a "wants" situation. In this case, it's not that your friend or family member wants to buy a new car or a pair of shoes; she wants to tell a story over and over. It's useful to think about this situation as if it were a classic want scenario and use the tools you've learned so far to probe deeper. You may even find a need or a value underneath all the reruns.

Some well-crafted questions for his situation could be: "What is this story really about?" "What does this story mean to you?" "What is telling this story getting you?" These will help her free herself from the story itself.

The second scenario that requires more work of you is when your partner never spontaneously brings up his past. This, of course, means something; what is not being said is just as significant as what *is* being said. When it comes to youth and childhood, it's pretty safe to assume there's more to the absence of storytelling than simple forgetfulness.

You can broach the subject of another person's past by simply noting that you've never heard him talk about it. I recommend not pushing the subject too hard if you feel substantial resistance. There's no need to turn exploring each other's worlds into a fight or an ultimatum.

Simply start with noticing and communicating to him what you've noticed (this is a bit of caring at work!). "I've noticed you never mention your parents. What's that about?" A simple observation plus a spacious invitation to share are often all another person needs.

If you still encounter substantial resistance — but you're committed to creating closeness with this person — the most you can do is continue to show up. Observe and invite whenever it seems appropriate. Over time, the act of showing up will build trust. The more you build trust, the more likely he will be to share his story.

If and when he does open up, and there's a lot of emotion, just be with him. Let him grieve if he needs to grieve. Let him be angry if he needs to be angry. This is a moment to return to the simplest thing you're trying to communicate: "I'm here with you. What would you like to say?" When it's over, he will remember that you were there for him.

Tips for talking about the past:

- Maintain an inviting mind-set.
- Engage in stories about the past when they arise naturally.
- Expect emotions! Don't shut them down — they are a natural part of the process.
- Ask yourself the questions you would ask if the story were a novel or movie.
- Learn to look through the other person's lens.
- Try predicting — you are no longer assuming!

Moment to Moment

As we wrap up our discussion of how to know someone for the purposes of getting closer, one important piece remains. It's directly tied to conversations about the past and future, but it's also fundamental for knowing in general. That piece is *reciprocity*.

We talked about reciprocity for a moment in the chapter about picking partners. I defined it there as the ability for your partner to both give you your moment as well as take her moment. You shine a light on her, and she shines a light on you.

So far we've concentrated on becoming excellent at giving someone else his moment. This includes our discussions of:

- Putting your assumptions aside to let your partner speak freely from her perspective
- Allowing her wants to mean something different from what your wants mean

- Investigating her needs and values
- Refraining from latching on to similarities to get closer

But it's just as important to take your moment when it's given to you. You must allow yourself to be on the receiving end of investigative questions, and you must answer them to the best of your ability, just as you expect your partner to do. At some point, you will need to share your story and let your partner be the one who listens. Closeness requires that you allow her access to your inner world as well.

This may sound obvious. Of course we both have to disclose our inner worlds to be able to mutually access them. But this is actually the point at which many, many relationships get tripped up. Just because both people should be the center of attention at certain times does not mean they should both be the center of attention *at once.*

Think of reciprocity as a tennis game. There's only one ball, and that ball is the center of attention. When the attention comes your way, you engage with it and then send it back. There's no stress or sense of loss in sending it back because you trust your partner will return it again in a minute. It's a game of mutual trust and understanding. Think of how ridiculous the game would be if both players were competing to hit the ball at the same time!

Because of all you've learned so far about knowing, you should be excellent at giving your partner the ball. You know how to give your partner her moment. So how do you take *your moment?*

The key is not to deflect. Be willing to do what you've been asking your partner to do this whole time: self-reflect, self-disclose, and go into the depths. There'll be more instruction on how to better access your own inner world (which is critical for getting close to someone else) in a later chapter. For now you simply need to understand that for you to take your moment, you must shine a light on your inner world.

Last, do your best not to confuse reciprocity with *reaction*. There'll inevitably be times when your partner says things that affect you, things that make you sad, frustrated, or angry. Resisting the urge to react is a challenge for everyone, but you should always try. Reacting is actually stealing your partner's moment, and that's always a mistake.

I once coached a couple in their midtwenties whom I'll call Ava and Nathan. They had been together for four years — since college — and had been living together for the past year. Everything was going well with them. During our sessions, they laughed a lot and showed great affection for each other.

They came to see me to help facilitate a conversation about what their future would look like together — just like what we've been talking about in this chapter. They were both unhappy in their jobs, and neither felt ready to get married. Although they had a great relationship, both felt a lot of anxiety about where it was heading.

I asked Nathan how he saw his future. He focused on the possibility of going to grad school to study the thing he really loved: journalism. He named the schools he'd most like to attend: Columbia, Northwestern, American University. He spoke with great passion and excitement about this life direction.

I could see that something was happening with Ava. She was listening — Nathan had clearly told her about this dream already — with her eyes fixed on the floor. She smiled sweetly at him when he touched her, but she didn't smile with her eyes. It was clear what was happening. None of the schools he dreamed of were in the Bay Area. They were all far away. What would happen to her? What would happen to *them*?

As Nathan recounted his vision, Ava was having her own experience. She was feeling the fear — maybe even panic — about him leaving. She was also feeling sadness...perhaps a little rejection. She sensed the relationship was being threatened.

While she didn't prevent herself from feeling her feelings, she did not express them while Nathan was talking. Because these two were skilled at reciprocity, she let him have his moment to be excited about his dream. As soon as he was done, he gave the moment right back to her.

"How are you doing over there?" he asked.

"I'm okay. I'm worried," she replied.

We then spent time delving into Ava's feelings about what Nathan had said and what she sees for her future.

This interaction is so elegant you'd hardly know there were any skills at play. But think of how a couple less fluent in reciprocity might have handled it. Nathan may not have told the truth about what he wanted (or told it with less honest excitement) because he feared Ava's reaction. As soon as Ava felt her sad and fearful feelings, she might have interrupted, given him a guilt trip, or disparaged his dream. Or Nathan might have kept talking about what he wanted, ad nauseam, unable to notice that his partner was suffering.

I want to make clear that Ava was not denying her feelings — she was absolutely feeling them — and she did express them when the time was right. She was simply waiting, just for a moment, because she understood that interrupting *would not actually work*. Interrupting might have felt good in the moment, but it would not get her more of what she wanted: closeness with Nathan.

To reap more closeness, she needed to give him his moment to be excited. As a result of her doing this, he felt heard and understood. Feeling heard and understood helped him feel ready to give the moment back to her and let her talk about how she was feeling sad and worried. If, however, Nathan had felt as if Ava had stolen his moment to be excited, he would have entered the conversation about her feelings begrudgingly. Then neither would have felt fully heard or understood, and both would have walked away feeling a little more distant.

Questions for Reflection

- What aspect of your past or future do you leave out when telling another person the story of your life?
- Do you find that the people around you tend to talk more about the future or more about the past? Do you like this tendency?
- Is there anyone in your life whose stories you'd like to know better? How might you engage with her about her life story?

 ## An Exercise to Challenge Yourself

Pick a character from your favorite book or movie. Write down a list of ten questions you'd like to ask him to understand more about his past or future. Make the questions specific to that character and what you already know about him. This will help you ask more person-specific, less general questions.

Chapter Summary

- Knowing someone in time is critical for creating closeness because our memories of the past and visions of the future are at the heart of our perspective of the present moment. The past and future are always with us.
- The past often lives in us as lessons learned. The future often lives in us as a drive for something better.
- Your partner's past, in particular, is useful to understand because it has shaped the lens through which she sees the world. If you can learn to see through this lens as well, you can predict how your partner will interpret things in real time.
- Reciprocity means being able both to give your partner

his moment and to take your own. Although you both get to have your moments, that does not mean you take moments *at the same time*. Reciprocity is like a tennis game — back and forth.

• Reciprocity is also not the same as reacting. Simply reacting to what your partner says may hijack her moment and create distance between the two of you.

Part 3

Mastering the Art of Caring

Chapter 9

Feeling Another Person's Feelings

When I worked in performance marketing at start-ups, I gained the reputation for having psychic abilities. Mind you, I am in no way psychic. But I am good at one thing that, frankly, I thought everyone could do: reading the room. Reading the room means being able to sense what's going on within a particular group of people. It's metacognition, an awareness of the undertone that always emerges when people get together. It's being able to tap into an emotional field. It's a feeling.

I first became known for this ability when I started attending weekly meetings with other teams. We, the various teams of the company, would sync up regularly to make sure we were all staying coordinated. These meetings were dry: I'm working on this; it'll be done by then. Hardly the stuff of magic.

But after these meetings, I would remark on how this person was frustrated with that person, how that person was probably going to quit soon, or how that person had something difficult going on at home.

"How do you know that?" my boss would ask.

"I don't know. I thought it was obvious," I'd reply.

The truth is, I knew these things about my coworkers because

I was picking up on subtle emotional cues. I could sense — without really realizing it — clusters of feelings in others and tie them correctly to a particular emotion. I was *empathizing*. As surprised as my coworkers were that I could do this, I was just as surprised that they *couldn't*. I thought everyone could feel people's feelings!

Since I've become a relationship coach, I've learned that empathizing can be a real challenge if it doesn't come naturally. I've also happily learned that this is not an insurmountable challenge. If sensing emotions in others doesn't come to you naturally, you can absolutely learn how to do it. This chapter will provide you with a simple framework.

And why *should* you learn to empathize with other people's feelings? Because this skill is essential to the act of *caring*. As we move out of our discussion of knowing another person and into caring about him or her, there is no other place to start but with feelings. When you notice a barely perceptible frown cross a coworker's face and feel a pang of sadness yourself, that's your first indication that you care about her well-being. When you see a flash of amazement cross your father's face at his surprise party and you beam at him in return, this is caring brought to life.

Feelings are the gateway through which one passes from knowing about another person's inner world to wanting to keep that world safe, healthy, and vibrant. Let's learn how feelings draw you closer to others — and farther away from loneliness.

The Benefits and Pitfalls of Feelings

I doubt you need much convincing that feelings are a central component of caring and, by extension, of closeness. If you know only intellectually that you *should* be close to someone or *should* care about him, the relationship feels hollow. A relationship that lacks genuine feelings can become a chore. Purely rational relationships

— ones with no emotional connection — certainly do have their place in the world...when they serve as a practical means to an end. But they are not ends in and of themselves; they do not produce the experience of closeness. We call it *feeling close* for a reason.

To put a finer point on it, feelings are what make a relationship feel *authentic*. If you believe the other person cares about your well-being not because she's supposed to but because she's genuinely driven from her heart to care, you will not question the closeness that springs from this caring. It will feel sincere and natural. It will feel *real*.

This much likely seems obvious to you. But perhaps you're wondering, "Why exactly does *empathizing* matter so much in the realms of caring and closeness?" The answer to that question is also straightforward, when we're reminded what closeness is: direct access to another person's inner world. When you feel another person's feelings — when you empathize — you're gaining access to her emotional world. Moving beyond her purely cerebral world, empathizing allows you to touch — to literally feel — the terrain of her emotional landscape.

Stated another way, when you empathize, you learn about more than just her needs, values, and stories. You'll feel how much she longs for her needs to be met. You'll feel the passion she has for her values. You'll feel the pain underlying her childhood stories. You'll learn more than just the facts — you'll sense what *matters* about the facts.

Having little to no access to your partner's emotional world makes feeling close nearly impossible, no matter how much you objectively know about him. This would be like reading the lyrics to a song without hearing the music. You would know what the song was saying, but you would develop no connection with it. You would comprehend the content, but it would have no power over you. You would *get it*, but you wouldn't *care*.

To really care about another person, you must feel her feelings. Before we dive into the how's, let's take a look at one complication that tends to be a huge pitfall for people in relationships.

Although empathizing is essential to closeness, it's not a given that feeling another person's feelings *always* brings you closer. Empathizing is not foolproof. For example, if you feel your partner's frustration with you, you may react fearfully and pull away. If you sense him lacking interest in you, you may retreat. If you pick up on her anger and feel threatened, you may pick a fight. In other words, empathy brings people closer together, but if mismanaged, it can also drive people apart.

Empathizing, in the way we usually understand it, can be unruly. You may have found that the unfortunate instances when feeling your partner's feelings creates distance instead of closeness are hard to control. These instances are hard for *everyone* to control. That's because, in a very real sense, we all have two separate brains: a thinking brain and a feeling brain. The structures that comprise the thinking brain — specifically the neocortex — and those that comprise the feeling brain — the limbic system and specifically the amygdala — are usually beautifully in sync... until something highly emotional happens.

When your feeling brain gets aroused because it feels threatened, for example, it can (and does) take over the thinking brain entirely. Daniel Goleman describes these "limbic hijackings" in his groundbreaking book *Emotional Intelligence*: "At those [highly emotional] moments, evidence suggests, a center in the limbic brain proclaims an emergency, recruiting the rest of the brain to its urgent agenda. The hijacking occurs in an instant, triggering this reaction crucial moments before the neocortex, the thinking brain, has had a chance to glimpse fully what is happening, let alone decide if it is a good idea."

What this means for you in your journey out of loneliness is that feeling a friend's feelings is wonderful... until he feels something (anger, disgust, even sadness) that triggers an intense negative emotion in you. In these moments you are primed to get limbically hijacked, become irrational, and say or do things that ultimately create more distance than closeness.

Fortunately, there is a way to overcome this physiological reality and harness empathy to produce more positive results (closeness) than negative (distance). The solution I offer is to *empathize deliberately*. This means intentionally slowing down the process of empathizing so your thinking and feeling brains can get coordinated again.

While perhaps you've been thinking of empathizing as a single event, for the purposes of creating closeness, empathizing deliberately is a *process* comprised of three events. Consciously performing each step in the process slows down your reaction rate, gives you time to soothe yourself, and allows more information to make it out of your feeling brain and into your thinking brain. This process will allow you to feel deeply while remaining rational:

1. Recognize and identify the other person's feelings.
2. Feel that same feeling in yourself.
3. Respond in a way that communicates caring.

When you empathize deliberately, you'll consistently gain access to your partner's emotional inner world — which is necessary for closeness — regardless of what you find there, whether it be scary, sad, depressing, or discomfiting. Empathizing deliberately works in the service of closeness and will produce better results than just feeling and reacting. Let's learn how to perform each step of this process well.

Step 1. Recognize and Identify the Other Person's Feelings

The first step in the process of empathizing deliberately is to recognize and correctly identify a feeling in another person. You do this primarily through observation. As I mentioned at the beginning of the book, caring is essentially the same thing as noticing.

Most people provide clues about what they're feeling through their facial expressions, voice tone, gestures, and so on. When you notice these emotional cues in another person, you begin down the path of correctly identifying his or her feelings.

You already notice some of these cues and know what they look like: your mom has tension in her voice, your sister's eyebrows are furrowed, your cofounder is relentlessly rubbing his hands together. These signals are floating around us all the time and, for most of us, it's intuitive to pick up on them. The challenge with noticing these cues is: What do they actually *mean?*

Does the tension in your mom's voice mean she's stressed out or excited? Is your sister angry or just focused? Is your cofounder happy or about to run out of the room? It can often be challenging to jump the chasm from noticing a cue to identifying the feeling that's behind it.

To help you make this leap, let's first establish how many feelings people actually have. Traditionally there were thought to be seven fundamental emotions: anger, contempt, disgust, happiness, sadness, fear, and surprise. New research suggests there may be as few as four: anger/contempt/disgust, happiness, sadness, and fear/surprise. For simplicity's sake, let's maintain that there are four major emotional states: mad, glad, sad, and afraid.

These are the four states you want to familiarize yourself with and learn to identify in another. The emotional cues you pick up from someone will likely lead you down one of these four paths. Luckily, each emotion has its own hallmarks. Here are the archetypal expressions of the four emotional states:

Mad

- Fists clenched
- Jaw clenched with tight lips
- Eyebrows pulled down and drawn together
- Loud or stressed voice
- Quick gestures, especially in hands
- Lip curl (signifies disgust)
- Eye roll (signifies contempt)

Glad

- Body-wide relaxation
- Smiling with the mouth and the eyes
- Laughter
- Good-natured joking
- Increased energy
- Head nodding
- Open hands and body position
- Eye contact (signifies interest)

Sad

- Watery eyes or crying
- Eyebrows furrowed or collapsed
- Frowning
- Sighing
- Softening of the voice
- Overall decrease in energy
- Slumped-over or crumpled body position

Afraid

- Paleness in the face
- Lips stretched toward the ears and eyebrows raised and drawn together

- Eyelids widened to take in more information
- Voice pitched higher than normal
- Fidgeting
- Holding one's breath
- Tense or straight-up body position

These hallmarks are a great place to start in identifying your partner's feelings. Moreover, if you see your partner expressing more than one hallmark at the same time (for example, sighing *and* slumping over *and* watery eyes), you can feel confident you are on the road to identifying the right emotion (in this case, sadness).

While it's critical to be conscious of the hallmarks of each emotion, you can be led astray if you take any one of these indicators too literally. A college friend of mine had a habit of air-punching the walls of his apartment with his fists when people came over. According to our list of hallmarks, clenched fists — and assumedly thrown jabs — means anger, right?

That's what I thought when I first saw him do this; I thought he had a serious anger problem. But as I got to know him, I learned that he was a boxing enthusiast and the air-punching did not indicate anger at all. I visited him one time at his boxing gym and watched him throw his fists, happy as a clam, for an hour straight. For him, punching meant excitement, not aggression, and this cue would more appropriately fall in the "glad" category. When we came over, he threw fists because he was happy to see us!

Keep in mind three points when it comes to identifying emotions in others through observation. First, don't take any one cue in isolation. Sure, my friend had clenched fists, but was he also smiling cheerily at the same time? Was he also laughing? The more cues you observe and gather, the better sense you'll have of what the other person is feeling.

Second, always read cues in the context of the situation. Throwing fists in a boxing gym has a completely different meaning from throwing fists in your boss's office. Take into account what would be normal in any given situation, and then notice outliers from there.

Third, read cues based on what you know about the person. If I'd known from the beginning that my friend was into boxing, I would likely have known that for him, fists are equated with a good mood. This is one of the reasons the knowing chapters come first in this book. The information you learn while getting to know each other will help you feel each other's feelings more accurately and, by extension, will help you care about each other more effectively.

Step 2. Feel That Same Feeling in Yourself

Once you've correctly identified your partner's emotions, it's time for step 2: feeling that same feeling in yourself. This is not a mental or intellectual pursuit, it's a physical one. You need to feel — in your body — what the other person is feeling. If he's thrilled, you get your own little rush of adrenaline. If she's stressed out, you get a surge of cortisol yourself. If he's blissful, you flood with dopamine as well.

This step is profoundly important to the process of empathizing deliberately, because physically feeling what the other person is experiencing prevents your body from having its own, separate, reactionary feeling. For example, let's say your mom is sad about selling her home, but you think she should be over it by now. The house has been on the market for more than a year and, in your opinion, she has had plenty of time to grieve.

You could perform the first step of the empathizing process well and identify that she is sad, but if you don't correctly perform this second step — feeling that same feeling in yourself — you may end up feeling angry or frustrated at her sadness. You're sick of her sadness! While this is a common way to react in such a situation, your anger or frustration is just that — a reaction. Moreover, it's a reaction that will create more distance between you and your mom. If, instead, you allow yourself to have a mutual moment of sadness with her, this negative emotion will bring the two of you closer.

The importance of this middle step does not just make intuitive sense; it's also been proven. Starting in 1980, research psychologist John Gottman brought married couples into his lab and asked them to fight about a perpetual problem in their relationship; he both monitored their physiology and videotaped them. He then asked each partner to watch the videotape and, using a dial, rate how the other person was feeling throughout the fight.

The results of this study speak volumes about the value of physically feeling another person's feelings. Those who could most accurately indicate what their spouse was feeling while watching the video were those who were physically *feeling the same thing*. Their emotional states mirrored the emotional states of their partner. When the spouses' physiology reflected each other's feelings, the fight was found to be less damaging to the relationship in the long run. When their physiology failed to make this shift, the fight was far more damaging.

Feeling in your body what your partner feels reduces distance in and of itself. Beyond that, it allows you to really know what the other person is experiencing — to have direct access to her emotional inner world. This direct access increases closeness *and* helps you discern how best to respond in a way that communicates caring. Since you've put yourself in her place emotionally, you can ask yourself, "What would make me feel better if I was feeling that way? What would be comforting? What would make me feel worse?" These questions lead you into the third step of empathizing deliberately: responding in a way that communicates caring.

Step 3. Respond in a Way
That Communicates Caring

This third step — responding to the other person's emotion in a way that communicates caring — takes empathy beyond the realm of noticing what's going on and into the realm of communicating that you *care about* what's going on. Up until this point, you have cared about her well-being. Here, in the third step, is where you *show her* you care.

While there is no script for communicating caring, there are ways to respond to another person's feelings that work to move you two toward closeness. First, use the experience of feeling her feeling yourself to discern what response would have felt caring *to you* in that moment. When you felt your mom's sadness as she was leaving her home, what response to that sadness would have made *you* feel cared about had you been in her shoes? Would it have felt caring to have someone hold your hand? Would it have felt caring if someone had changed the subject? Run through a few options in your mind, and select one that you sense would have brought you closer to the person responding in that way. You can't be sure it'll be the perfect response — some people love physical comfort, while others don't, for example — but you can be sure it'll be a thoughtful response.

This technique — imagining what would have felt caring to you had you been in the other person's shoes — is extremely useful for crafting caring responses. It will be your main guidepost for responding to your partner's emotion in a way that communicates caring. But often it can be challenging to think this clearly when you're just coming off a strong emotion yourself. If you find yourself not being able to think of a response that would have worked for you, remember one simple rule: respond "soft" to soft emotions and "hard" to hard emotions.

Soft emotions are those that make the other person more

open, receptive, and vulnerable to you. These usually congregate around happiness and sadness (the emotional states of glad and sad). Examples of soft emotions include joy, regret, remorse, admiration, trust, grief, and pain. Hard emotions, on the other hand, are the ones that make your partner less open, less receptive, and less vulnerable to you. These center on anger, fear, disgust, contempt, jealousy, and worry (the mad and afraid states).

When your partner is experiencing a soft emotion, her walls naturally come down and make her inner world more available to you. For this reason, it's usually best to simply *be with her* in her soft state, since you actually need to do very little to become closer in this state. When feelings are soft, less is more. In the case of your mom's sadness about leaving her home, she was experiencing a soft emotion, and she likely would have interpreted the least invasive response — the softest response — as the most caring.

Hard emotions, on the other hand, tend to build up protective walls around the person feeling them. Anger and fear are defensive feelings, usually triggered by a perceived threat. These emotions, gone unchecked, draw people away from one another because the emotional walls that they produce get higher and higher the more the hard emotion is reinforced. In other words, stewing in anger tends to make people angrier. Dwelling in worry tends to make people more worried. Wallowing in jealousy only makes someone more jealous.

For this reason, the most caring response to a hard emotion is typically a hard response, that is, one that challenges the veracity of the feeling. This may be surprising to you, given what you know about the negative effects of challenging another person's inner world. Usually, we accept whatever the other person shares about her inner world as truth, right? Right. So let's be clear: a hard response — one that challenges the emotion — does not mean you're telling the other person that she is wrong for feeling anger, worry, or jealousy. It means you believe there is something more beneath the anger, worry, or jealousy; it means you don't take the hard emotion at face value. A response that challenges is one that tries to dig deeper.

If your partner is feeling a hard emotion, it works well to ask some well-crafted questions in the same way you would to get to know her. Think of it like investigating wants. "What is this anger really about?" "What does this jealousy get you?" Standing up to hard emotions in this way helps the other person look within, investigate her own inner world, and tell you what she finds. And when she does, she will have more information about her inner world to share with you. In this way, a challenging response to a hard emotion communicates caring, increases access to the other person's inner world, and increases closeness.

If there's someone in your life you know a lot about, work with him to increase your understanding of each other's emotional worlds. You will feel instantly closer.

A Note about Technology and Feelings

You absolutely can get better at reading the room and feeling someone else's feelings. That being said, emotional awareness is one of the primary relationship skills that technology is making more difficult to hone. Emotional cues are lost when you interact with another person through a mediated device. Put simply, technology can hinder your progress toward empathizing well.

You likely know this to be true from your own experience with mediated interactions. I'd bet you've had a nice, calm conversation with someone over text... while you were secretly crying your eyes out or seething with anger. Perhaps you wanted your privacy in that moment and truly didn't want the other person to know you were crying or seething. But isn't this emotional disconnect inherently odd? Doesn't it blur the lines between what's "being together" and what's "being alone"?

We know intuitively that these types of interactions are strange, and now evidence has emerged showing that personal technology does indeed interrupt our ability to recognize emotions in each other. A recent study, led by UCLA professor of psychology Patricia Greenfield, sent a group of fifty-one sixth graders to camp for five days, where they had no access to technology. A second group of fifty-four sixth graders continued using their devices until they too were sent to the camp at a later date. The students were evaluated — both at the beginning and end of their time at camp — on their ability to correctly identify emotions in other people.

The results showed that increased technology use is related to decreased emotional awareness: "In the beginning, [the first group of kids] were unable to read the emotions in the photographs and videos accurately. But over the five-day period they improved drastically, they were able to read non-verbal cues, facial expressions better than those who were using their media devices and were yet to join the camp." By contrast, those who attended camp at a later date saw no improvement in their ability to recognize emotions.

When you're trying to get close, interact with the other person through a channel that provides the most information possible. That is true always — but it is never truer than when you are learning to feel your partner's feelings. Of course, face-to-face conversation is always the best choice; the emotional information available to you in real time is invaluable.

Questions for Reflection

- Do you consider yourself fluent in feelings? Do you easily notice feelings in others? Do you feel emotions intensely in yourself?
- Are you aware of any emotional cues you tend to give off? For example, do you sigh a lot? Are you always shaking your foot at work? What might these signals be conveying to others?
- What's one hard emotion you've been feeling lately? How could you go about challenging this emotion yourself?

An Exercise to Challenge Yourself

Use your downtime watching movies or TV to practice correctly identifying emotions. Keep a notebook beside you while you watch, and write down the emotions you read in the facial expressions and gestures of the actors. Better yet, watch with a friend who's doing the same, then compare lists after the show is over to see if you two were picking up the same cues.

Chapter Summary

- You need to feel your partner's feelings — to empathize with her — in order to access her emotional inner world. Feeling the other person's feelings is essential for building caring and closeness.
- However, if what you feel in your partner is somehow upsetting, threatening, or disturbing to you, it can cause you to retreat — creating more distance than closeness.
- The solution to this problem is to *empathize deliberately*. Empathizing deliberately is a three-step process:

1. Recognize and identify a feeling in another. This requires familiarizing oneself with observation and with the nonverbal cues that give emotions away.

2. Feel that same feeling in yourself. This is not a mental or intellectual pursuit; it's physical. Physically feeling the other person's feeling prevents you from feeling your own, reactionary feeling instead.

3. Respond in a way that communicates caring. Use your experience of feeling your partner's feeling to imagine what would have made you feel better in her position. And remember, when a soft emotion arises, simply be there with your partner. When a hard emotion arises, challenge it.

Chapter 10

Uniting as a Team

While feelings are a central component to caring, caring is not an entirely emotional experience. There's also an intellectual component to caring, a mental stance that one must maintain to create lasting closeness. This stance is that your partner is fully human.

I wouldn't blame you if you giggled a little when you read that. You're probably thinking, "The technology mind-set hasn't taken over so much that I don't know other people are human!"

Of course you know that other people are human. But I bet you forget all the time. You forget when you have to ask your husband fourteen times to take out the trash. You forget when your best friend's had one too many drinks and humiliates you. You forget when your brother's in one of his neurotic, anxious states. You forget when your business partner is depressed and doesn't know why.

Remembering that your partner is human through and through is a conscious action, just like knowing and caring are. It's a stance — a frame of mind — that you actively hold, even when it's difficult. Even when it's hard to remember why you're doing it, you keep doing it. Why? Because you both reap profound benefits from honoring each other's humanity. Holding this level of respect for each other is the first step toward becoming a true *team*.

Viewing another person as human is the same thing as being able to recognize humanity in him or her. Humanity means that your partner, like you, belongs to the collective human family. This extremely simple fact is an important starting point because in it lies one of the most useful resources for creating closeness: realizing that other people are a lot like you.

I'll talk much more about this in the next chapter. For now suffice it to say that our membership in the human family makes us all naturally relatable.

Tradition insists that humans have a higher purpose on earth than other living things. This can be expressed in many different ways: We have much higher intelligence than most other animals; we are able to create things that animals can't. We can feel compassion and empathy. We can imagine transcending the material world and, potentially, our consciousness can *actually* transcend the material world. We have spirit; we have a soul.

However you like to frame it, being human is inextricably intertwined with being precious. When you're remembering the humanity of your partner, you're reaffirming that, yes, she is special and precious, just like all human life is. She is not thrown out of the human family just because she's being annoying right now.

But there is a flip side to the term *humanity*. We are special and valuable, but we are also deeply flawed. "I'm only human" is synonymous with "I'm weak" or "I messed up." Humanity means having the potential to be transcendent, but it is also means being all-but-fated to make mistakes.

These three aspects of humanity are essential to keep in mind when you're learning how to care about another person well: your partner is like you, she is inherently precious, and she will mess up. Holding this viewpoint allows us to care about another person fully and honestly as another human.

Separate the Person from the Problem

Once you've adopted the frame of mind that the person with whom you're creating closeness is human, the first thing you *do* to start treating him as a full human is to separate the person from the problem.

I first learned about this notion in the context of business negotiation. As Roger Fisher describes in his influential negotiation guide, *Getting to Yes*, "Dealing with a substantive problem and maintaining a good working relationship need not be conflicting goals if the parties are committed and psychologically prepared to treat each separately on its own legitimate merits."

I see the idea of separating the person from the problem as much more than just a negotiation technique. To me, it's the essence of the mental perspective of caring about someone. Separating the person from the problem means that your partner is not the same as her overeating, her lateness, or her shyness, and that she is not the same as the problems in the relationship that her partner might typically chalk up to being "her fault."

We conflate people with problems so much that we hardly understand the difference. This tendency is much more pervasive than we realize. Look at how we speak about people in normal life. Sandy sometimes shows up to meetings late, so Sandy *is* irresponsible. Sarah usually takes charge of the situation, so Sarah *is* controlling.

This happens in all contexts. Our adult children aren't where we thought they would be at their age, so they *are* lazy. Our team is going to miss our deadline *because of* our art director. I have a guest sleeping over at my house every night because my husband *is* codependent.

I've seen evidence in my work that we as a culture are starting to realize that this is an unproductive way of talking about other people. There is psychological evidence as well. Research done on couples indicates that those who are happiest in their relationships tend to separate their spouse from problems organically, without knowing they're "supposed" to: "A growing body of research is beginning to suggest that some relationship experiences, such as intimacy, may be largely in the eye of the beholder. For example, it is now well known that happily married couples tend to attribute undesired, negative spouse behavior to situational characteristics rather than to specific, dispositional characteristics of the spouse (Bradbury & Fincham, 1990)."

So what does "attribute[ing] undesired behavior to situational characteristics" actually look like? Let's return to the simple examples above.

1. Our adult children aren't where we thought they would be at their age, so they are lazy.
2. Our team is going to miss our deadline because of our art director.
3. I have a guest sleeping over at my house every night because my husband is codependent.

What are some other ways to present these scenarios?

1. My adult children are human; and my expectations of how their lives would progress turned out to be inaccurate.
2. My team's art director is human; and we didn't anticipate all the delays to getting this project done.
3. My husband is human; and I'm not getting any personal space in my house.

Notice how all these statements use the word *and*, not *but*. Both parts of the statement can be true at the same time. We can be humans, and there can be problems.

Separating the person from the problem isn't just a philosophical concept, and it's not as simple as just being compassionate. You're not just doing this to be nice. There are very practical reasons to think this way.

What does viewing the above situations in these new ways allow us to do? It allows us to continue being close to our adult children while consciously reevaluating our expectations. It allows us to continue showing our art director respect while committing to make more accurate timetables going forward. It allows us to continue to love and admire our husband while making changes to provide ourselves with more personal space.

Separating the person from the problem allows us to go easy on the person and hard on the problem. This is a profound shift. We no longer need to be trapped in the conundrum of whether we should treat the person who's "disappointing us" or "upsetting us" nicely or sternly — whether we should show him love or tough love... or just yell, intimidate, and cajole.

Always treat the person with love. Always treat the problem as if you're determined to destroy it.

The challenge of separating the person from the problem is being able to notice — and resist — the compulsion to meld *things he does* with *who he is*. As discussed in the knowing chapters, we very rarely know the reasons why one does what he does, unless we make the concerted effort to understand. So how can it be right to construct "who he is" from *our* experience of what he's doing?

Problems are real. Sometimes problems do arise from your partner's actions. But distance inevitably creeps into a relationship when you start attributing that problem to a character flaw in that person. It becomes increasingly more difficult to care about a person whose *inherent self* you see as problematic.

The Team vs. the Problem

There is another significant benefit to separating your partner from the problem: once the problem is considered separate from either of you, the two of you can *work together* to destroy it. The team now has two symbiotic incentives: to remain a close, united team and to utterly demolish the problem. With your incentives aligned, you can put all your energy into defeating the problem... as opposed to defeating your partner, whom you are trying to be close to.

Let's think about how two people who view each other as at least part of the problem try to solve a mutual problem. Usually, they compromise. One person attempts to change a little, and the other attempts to change a little. Both get some of what they want but also have to relinquish some of what they want.

Close friends, family members, couples, and business associates can do so much better than this. Compromising isn't ideal because it implies that the solution to the problem lies somewhere on a linear spectrum. If I get more of what I want, you get less of what you want. We have one lemon — if you get more lemon, I get less lemon. Someone ends up being the winner, while the other ends up the loser. This is not caring. We're not trying to make anyone the loser. We're trying to be less lonely!

Remember the lemon negotiation from earlier? The lemon meant something different to each partner; to one it meant a beverage, to the other it meant a cake. So when there's a problem — a disagreement, a fight, or tension of any kind — the first step toward demolishing it is to understand the deeper meaning of the presenting want. Use your investigation and question-asking skills.

Once the two of you fully understand what the problem is really about, you can come up with creative solutions (off the linear spectrum of "you get more, I get less") that genuinely satisfy both of you.

Let's look at the partnership of two men we'll call Josh and Tyler. Josh and Tyler were friends who founded a start-up together and also lived together. Josh liked to invite his friends over to the house every night. Tyler didn't feel particularly comfortable with it but figured being social was just "who Josh is." Josh, in return, assumed being antisocial was just "who Tyler is."

Not wanting to make either person change who he was, they had stopped trying to discuss this problem. Both actually thought they were being compassionate by not bringing it up, by not trying to make anyone change. But that didn't mean they weren't still unhappy with the situation — they both were. They just had no idea how to resolve it.

Over time, the tension this problem was causing started to affect their business. Something needed to be done. So Tyler took the first step and asked Josh a very spacious, nicely balanced question: "What is wanting to have friends over about for you?"

Josh revealed that his desire to have people over was less about the people themselves and more about finding a way to stop working. Once the friends came over, he felt justified in not working anymore that night. He and Tyler worked a lot...often all night. Sometimes Josh just needed to take a break, and the friends afforded him that.

Josh then returned the question: "What does avoiding the friend gatherings get you?" Interestingly, Tyler revealed he was actually yearning for the same thing — he simply expressed it in a different way. When he'd retreat to his room to avoid socializing, it was his way of taking a break. His version of taking a break simply didn't involve people.

Now they had gotten somewhere! The problem was not that "Josh is too social" or that "Tyler is too antisocial." They are both human, and they have a shared problem: they need to allow themselves to take breaks from working.

Knowing that, they could start coming up with solutions to the problem. As I'm sure you can see, there's no longer a linear spectrum of solutions here. The options were not just: Josh gets to have his friends over, Josh wins; Josh doesn't get to have his friends over, Tyler wins; or, Josh gets to have his friends over less frequently, and both guys win a little and lose a little.

They could instead come up with useful, creative, sustainable solutions that really address the underlying need. And because they're doing it together, they'll likely come up with a bigger, broader list of options than either would get to alone. Better yet, brainstorming can be a real bonding experience!

Maybe Josh starts going over to his friends' houses instead of inviting them to his. Maybe they agree to work no more than ten hours a day. Maybe they consider not living together anymore, so when they leave the office they're done for the night. There are endless possibilities for solutions. Solutions are only limited by the team's creative thinking.

Finally, my favorite aspect of this approach: flexibility. Both Josh and Tyler can now try out a variety of solutions until they find one that works. If they hadn't separated the people from the problem and had instead made one or the other the "loser," there'd be pressure on whatever compromise they came to. The person who "won" had better now make the other person's loss worth it.

In other words, if one partner wins and one partner loses, the winning partner had better stick to what he believed he wanted. Now the stakes are high. If he happens to find out that his solution doesn't really work, or he simply changes his mind, the other person's sacrifice was all for nothing. This is how resentments start to percolate...and resentments are a fierce enemy of caring.

Vulnerabilities Are Not Problems

I know what you're thinking. But what if the person really *is* the problem? I swear Jack is the problem. You should meet him; he's a jerk. Well, Jack probably isn't a person with whom you should create closeness...and that's totally fine. There's absolutely no reason to hitch your cart to someone you truly dislike.

But if you feel chronically lonely, or you're not getting close to anyone because you're waiting for someone who will never cause you a problem (or suffer a problem herself), you'll likely be waiting forever. Every person you'll ever attempt to be close to will have vulnerabilities.

Vulnerabilities are not the same as problems. Problems are circumstances — your irritable bowel syndrome or your five parking tickets — that if they were completely resolved, your life would be indisputably better.

Vulnerabilities, on the other hand, are aspects of a person that are typically hidden for fear of shame or rejection...but that does not make vulnerabilities bad. Something — a tendency, a preference — can be called a vulnerability if sharing it with another person feels risky. Vulnerabilities are indeed *not separate* from the person; they are part of being human.

That being said, vulnerabilities *can* contribute to problems. If one of your vulnerabilities is that you tend to have obsessive thoughts, it could indeed lead you into a problem, like maxing out your credit card. But these are still two separate things. Obsessiveness is your own, internal, human struggle. The maxed credit cards are a problem. If one of your vulnerabilities — let's say absentmindedness — causes you to miss a car payment, these are still two separate things. Absentmindedness is part of your human struggle. The missed car payment is a problem.

This should not be seen as letting people off the hook. Taking responsibility for your actions is undeniably important for creating closeness. It's one of the required abilities we discussed when learning to pick partners. But taking responsibility — in the way that really helps closeness flourish — means coming up with a solution that fixes the problem your vulnerability contributed to.

Taking responsibility for your obsessiveness would mean coming up with a plan to pay off your maxed-out credit cards, as well as taking action to make sure that doesn't happen again. Taking responsibility for your absentmindedness might mean arranging to have your car payments withdrawn from your bank automatically. Taking responsibility doesn't mean internalizing the problem — *I am the problem* — which does nothing but fill a person with shame. And shame only leads to more problems.

All people have vulnerabilities. Vulnerabilities are the essence of being human and must be welcomed when creating closeness. They do not discount any of your strengths. As researcher and vulnerability expert Brené Brown put it, "You're imperfect, and you're wired for struggle, but you are worthy of love and belonging."

When your partner's vulnerability does contribute to a problem, expect him to take responsibility for it and ensure it won't happen again. From there, make an effort to forgive.

Forgiveness, by my definition of the word, means forgiving the person, not the problem. The problem still needs to be resolved. But forgiveness is the ultimate form of going soft on a person. It's essential for caring about someone well because everyone makes mistakes. Your partner will have moments of carelessness and will sometimes fall short of her best self. Forgiveness *is* caring... when the other person needs it most.

Forgiving is just one way to show someone you care. There'll be much more to come regarding how to demonstrate caring to your partner. But the simplest, most essential thing you're doing when you care is paying attention. You are bearing witness.

There's a saying in meditation that you are not your thoughts. But if you're not your thoughts, who are you? You are the one who notices that the thoughts come and go. You are the witness.

This is exactly the case in relationships as well. In the closest relationships, you are simply paying attention, noticing, witnessing. Your partner's jobs come and go; he gains weight and loses weight. He breaks your favorite mug and then buys you two new ones. You show him you care by seeing it all come and go and continuing to witness his value and preciousness.

You are witness to his vulnerabilities with loving-kindness. You are witness to his triumphs, his failures. You stay attentively there — and neither of you is alone.

Questions for Reflection

- Is there someone in your life you often look at as a problem? How might you reframe your notion of this person to start humanizing him or her?
- Have you ever won a fight yet still felt as if you'd lost? What were the consequences of this "win"?
- What's one aspect of yourself that you usually hide? Would you consider this aspect a vulnerability? How might you start looking at it differently?

 An Exercise to Challenge Yourself

Pick a problem that's developed between you and another person — be it a disagreement, a stalemate, or an all-out battle. Invite that person to join you in a creative brainstorm of possible solutions to the problem. Remember: you're inviting the person onto your team, as your equal. The two of you, as a team, will combat the problem.

Chapter Summary

- Caring well requires holding a certain mental stance: that your partner is fully human. Three aspects of humanity are essential to keep in mind when learning to care well: your partner is like you, she is inherently precious, and she will mess up.

- The thing you actually *do* to honor your partner's humanity is to separate her as a person from her problems (and from the problems she creates within the relationship). This allows you to go easy on the person and hard on the problem. You can still treat your partner with love while resolving the problem.

- Once the problem is considered separate from either of you, the two of you can work together to destroy it. The team now has two symbiotic incentives: to remain a close, united team, and to utterly demolish the problem. With your incentives aligned, you can put all your energy into defeating the problem, as opposed to defeating each other.

- Vulnerabilities are not the same as problems. Problems are situations that if they were completely resolved, your life would be indisputably better. Vulnerabilities, on the other hand, are *part* of the person and should not be blamed for contributing to problems. The problem should be fixed; the person should be forgiven.

Chapter 11

Making a Relationship

When my husband and I were planning our wedding, the first thing we did was to open Google Docs and write down everything we could think of that was unique and special about our relationship. The first movie we watched together was *Face/Off*, so maybe that should play at the reception! We met doing advertising together, so maybe the place cards at dinner should be little ads! We both think bagpipes are the most hilarious of instruments, so maybe I should walk down the aisle to bagpipe music!

Truth be told, most of these ideas never made it into the wedding, but the list itself struck me as kind of awesome. This little document was a pretty accurate representation of everything that mattered about our relationship...at least metaphorically. One could look at it and see what we considered unique about our relationship — what we mutually valued, what we remembered about "our story," what we had created together.

We know how to care about someone at the most fundamental levels. We know how to feel someone else's feelings, how to respond to those feelings appropriately, how to recognize another person as fully human, and how to separate her from problems.

We know that our partner is precious and that her well-being matters to us.

These are the basic mental and emotion stances from which you start to care about another person. But there's more — much more.

To create a caring relationship with someone, you must create just that — a relationship. In our culture, we use the word *relationship* in all kinds of contexts to mean all kinds of things. But when it comes to closeness, a relationship has a very specific definition: a relationship is an entity that exists separate from either person but contains everything the people involved share. A relationship is not unlike that list of wedding ideas.

The metaphor of relationship-as-a-shared-document is actually quite useful in understanding this definition. If a relationship were a *Wikipedia* article (controlled by no one but generated through the efforts of many), it would be a constantly evolving, constantly improving collaborative creation of many. It would include the best that everyone had to offer, and the worst would, over time, get edited out.

You may have noticed that this chapter is titled "Making a Relationship" and not "Getting into a Relationship" or "Starting a Relationship." A relationship is not something that happens to you; it is something you create. Making a relationship is an action, just like knowing and caring are. It is a constant effort, something the two of you are always working on. It's a product that never ships.

A relationship is collaboration at its most powerful. As Clay Shirky explains in his sociological review of technology, *Here Comes Everybody*, "Collaborative production is simple: no one person can take credit for what gets created, and the project could not come into being without the participation of many."

For a relationship to be fully satisfying to both parties, it must be viewed this way. Why does this distinction — making a relationship vs. having a relationship happen to you — matter? Because highly caring relationships run the risk of challenging your identity. Caring deeply about another person can imply caring about him or her *more* than you care about yourself. If you think of a relationship as something that happens to you, as a new identity to take on, the relationship can quickly become an uncomfortable place to be.

Social science literature backs this up: "One's identity may be threatened if distinctions between self and other become unclear.... Stierlin (1976) suggests that the ability to differentiate between self and other is most likely to break down when trying to establish closeness or empathy. It seems possible that individuals may be able to tolerate only a certain degree of this inability to differentiate between self and others. When this threshold is crossed, the self may feel too close to the other."

In other words, when you start seeing yourself as *one person* with your partner, you may very quickly want to retreat. Losing yourself feels threatening, so the "we are one person" mind-set often backfires. This is the point at which one or both partners might start to pull away. And pulling away after closeness has already been established is one of the saddest and loneliest experiences a person can have.

So remember: a relationship is a *separate entity* from either of you. It is something the two of you create, but it is not a new identity. The two of you fill the shared document with all your unique trademarks — you both make it everything that it is — but neither of you *are* the shared document. Understanding relationships from this perspective allows you to make yours as caring as possible without losing yourself in the closeness.

How to Make a Relationship

One fundamental thing to understand about the relationship-as-separate-entity is that the relationship will have capabilities and knowledge beyond that of the individuals who comprise it. This may sound odd at first, but it becomes clear when applied to our metaphor of the shared document: a well-crafted *Wikipedia* article contains more knowledge of the topic discussed than any of the individual contributors do.

But for the *Wikipedia* article to work, it must be organized in a certain way. At the very least, the words must be oriented in a way that makes sense — that can be read and understood. In the same way, people must orient themselves in a certain way for the relationship to work, to make sense.

There are two absolutely essential orientations for a long-lasting, deeply caring, and satisfying relationship: relating and equality. Let's dive into the first one.

Relating is generally defined as being able to see yourself in someone else. You see a character in a movie, and if he looks like you, thinks like you, or acts like you, you relate to him. This definition, in my opinion, is not terribly useful. It makes it sound as if relating just happens haphazardly, as if whenever another person says something that sounds like something you'd say, you relate to him.

A more useful definition of *relating* is "being able to see *your humanity* in someone else through the reciprocal act of sharing human experiences." You share your experience of life with your partner, and you accept her experience of life as she offers it. These acts extend beyond simple talking and listening because the flow of sharing and accepting human experiences implies, "I see myself in you not because you look, act, or think like me, but because we are both human."

Relating, in the sense of sharing your humanity, your human

experiences, is the first step in creating the kind of unity that makes a relationship. "We are both human. I can see how you are precious *and* flawed, like me. I can see my good qualities in you, and I can see your bad qualities in me." This is how you intentionally, through action (not happenstance), get that feeling of seeing yourself in someone else.

Accepting the other person's human experiences and perspectives is necessary for relating well, yet it can be quite difficult to do. It's amazing how frequently we jump to challenge another person's thoughts, feelings, preferences, and interpretations. Just because these things are intangible doesn't mean they're not real to the other person.

Let's go back to the Google Doc my husband and I made for our wedding. Challenging the other person's perspective would be like my erasing all the content he contributed. This is in fact what we're doing when we try to talk our partners out of their thoughts, feelings, and perspectives — we are rewriting their content. I think you can see why this would be problematic. The more this happens, the more the other person gets lost, the more likely he is to feel his identity being threatened and to suddenly pull away.

Challenging your partner's perspective might make you more "right," but it sure doesn't make you less lonely.

If either one of you has had a certain experience or maintains a particular perspective, the relationship has it too. If he wants to write something in the shared document, it goes in the shared document. You can't censor each other and have a truly caring relationship.

Why "You" Doesn't Work

As we've established, language matters. In the same way that *why* is the word of interrogation and defensiveness, *you* is the word of separateness and poor relating. When starting a conversation about the relationship (or about something the other person is doing that makes you unhappy), choosing to start your sentence with "you" is the fastest way to get her to stop listening.

- "You are being too stubborn."
- "You are smothering me."
- "You need to stop speaking to me that way."

"You" is detrimental to relating well because it's calling out the other person's separateness — "you" do things that "I" don't. And if you do things that I don't, doesn't that imply that I see you as slightly less human than me? Moreover, it's very difficult to start a sentence with "you" and not conflate the person with the problem.

The better way to bring up possibly divisive topics for discussion (while maintaining maximum caring) is to speak from your own reality. Speaking from a place of "I" — how the situation is affecting you — is a more accurate place to talk from because you have legitimate knowledge of your experience; you don't have legitimate knowledge of "how she's being" or "what she needs to be doing."

The above phrases, redone as "I" statements, could look like:

- "I would like to come up with a solution we can both be happy about."
- "I need to have more space for myself."
- "I can't really hear the meaning of your words when they're said so aggressively."

Using "I" statements has great benefits, the first of which is that it's a way to express your perspective while still maintaining — enhancing, even — the unity of the relationship. You're adding more to the shared document — making it more complete and robust. Expressing your perspective and having it accepted is what relating is all about, after all.

The second great benefit is that your statements will be significantly less threatening to your partner. You can get your point across without implying that he's doing something wrong...or *being someone who's wrong.*

Last, there's a very subtle benefit to using "I" instead of "you." "I" statements are actually much harder for the other person to refute than "you" statements. Your partner will feel much less compelled to talk you out of an "I" statement — especially if she sees you as completely human — and will likely just accept what you're saying. This means you're actually *more likely* to win if you choose not to play the game at all.

How to Be Equals

The second stance that's essential for creating a great relationship is to treat each other as equals. We may think we treat our partner as an equal already, but this is a much subtler task than it appears. Anytime you come from a place of superiority — of knowing more about your partner's life experience than she does — you're not treating her as an equal.

Treating each other as equals requires a certain amount of trust — trust that you both know your own life experiences better than anyone else does. Trust means that you believe the other person can manage his own life better than anyone else can. In other words, trust and autonomy go hand in hand.

Equality in the sense that I'm using it — being autonomous peers who choose to make a relationship together — is a tactic used in all kinds of successful relationships. The concepts of equality, trust, and autonomy are not relegated to the realms of romance and marriage. They are becoming guiding principles in the business world too.

In 2013 a company called Supercell was considered the most

exciting game company around. An article about the company ran on *Forbes*'s website with the title "Is This the Fastest Growing Game Company Ever?" The company wasn't exciting for industry insiders just because it was making $2.5 million a day at the time; it was also the unique structure of the company itself, a tribute to radical equality in business, that made it so intriguing.

CEO Ilkka Paananen described himself as "the world's least powerful CEO." A prominent investor summarized Supercell's structure as such: "As its name implies, Supercell is organized as a collection of small, independent teams called cells tasked with developing new games or building new deep features for existing games. Cells are given complete autonomy in terms of how they organize themselves, prioritize ideas, distribute work and determine what they ultimately produce. . . . Ilkka encourages cells to exercise extreme independence and prides himself on having no creative control over them once they are constituted. The company as a whole is merely an aggregation of these cells; a Supercell."

It would not be a stretch to think of "Supercell" as the relationship and the "cells" as the independent partners who create it. No one dictates to the cells what to do, and everyone — the collective — shares in the gains.

I see Supercell's structure as equality in practice. The CEO does not come from a place of superiority. He trusts that the individual teams are capable of contributing to the whole, of being responsible and productive, and of solving their own problems.

Advice about Advice

Equality is a sweeping concept, to be sure. But there is a specific way in which we frequently fail to treat our partner as an equal: by giving advice.

There is certainly a time and a place for giving advice: when you're an expert in a certain field, when you're a teacher or consultant, and so forth. But within relationships — where the two parties creating the relationship are equals — advice fosters distance. Advice fosters loneliness.

You can't give unsolicited advice to a close friend, family member, life mate, or business associate without implying, "I understand the situation better than you do." However subtle, this is a stance of superiority. This is the mentality of "I'm the CEO so I understand your project better than you do…even though you're the one working on it." Anyone who's been on the receiving end of that kind of attitude knows how divisive — and straight-up infuriating — it can be.

Let's take a closer look at the downsides of giving advice.

Cynthia comes home after a tough day at work and wants to talk to her husband, Patrick, about how her boss is treating her unfairly. Patrick wants to be helpful and tells her all these things she should try to do differently. Cynthia probably agrees with some of the suggestions and disagrees with others but generally leaves the conversation feeling annoyed and doesn't know why.

It's likely she's at least partially annoyed because she didn't get to fully share her feelings about the situation with Patrick. She may be feeling emotionally shut down. This is important, but the failure of this interaction doesn't end there.

In addition, by giving her advice about what she should do differently, Patrick: (1) conflated her with the problem — "you should be different" and (2) implied that he understood the situation better than she did, even though he's *farther removed* from the situation than she is. The first part is a failure of humanity; the second is a failure of equality.

This scenario may seem relatively innocuous. After all, what damage can a little bit of advice do? In reality, the advice itself likely won't do much damage to the relationship. But it's the *place you're coming from* when you give unwanted advice — a place of superiority — that can be genuinely disastrous for relationships.

It's the same frame of mind we have when we start feeling contempt for our partner. *Contempt* means viewing another person as below one's consideration, as worthless, or as deserving of scorn. This is an extreme form of coming from a place of superiority. And contempt is an absolute pox on relationships. Contempt is very likely the most destructive feeling one person can feel for another.

The other problematic part of advice is that it's stealthy. We do it so much more often than we realize, unconsciously creating distance all around us. If you're talking to a friend who's expressing concern about something and you start your response with "All you need to do is…" "You need to realize that…" "Couldn't you just…" or "What if you tried…," you're giving advice.

You probably think you're just sharing your perspective on the situation, but your partner will receive it as "I know more about what you should be doing than you do." This instantly provokes her to defend her status as "the one who knows more."

These are the reasons to be very careful about giving advice to those you want to be close to. I want to reiterate that advice is not in and of itself bad. Advice is absolutely helpful sometimes. So how do you know when you *should* give advice?

If someone is seeking your expertise in a matter you're very knowledgeable about — asking you to be a consultant, in a sense — you should absolutely give advice. But this person is most likely not interacting with you because he wants to be close to you. That makes it a different interaction entirely.

Is there ever a time to give advice to someone you *are* trying to be close to? Yes. It's just way less frequent than you might think. Give advice only when your partner says the words "I'd like your advice on…" This boundary can easily be something you design into the relationship — something you write in your shared document. You'll certainly mess up sometimes and accidentally give unwanted advice, but your frame of mind when it comes to the other person will be much more caring.

And really, if you're not sure whether or not to give advice, just don't. People are inundated with advice and will not mind having a little less of it. You'll never hear one spouse turn to the other and say, "Honey, I really wish you'd give me more advice."

If you really, truly can't keep the advice from spilling out of your mouth regularly, at the very least, restate your partner's view on the situation to her satisfaction before giving the advice. Better yet, restate twice, then give advice! This at least lets her know that you've really heard her and creates a nice "knowing" buffer for the advice to fall on.

Modeling and Mirroring

There's a much better way to guide another person in the direction you think will best help him (which is really the purpose of advice in the first place): modeling. Modeling means setting an example of the traits and/or behaviors you'd like your partner to show more (or less) of. It's like writing in the shared document in a very elegant style, having your partner read your writing, and say, "I want to write like that too!"

Let's go back to Cynthia and Patrick for a minute. He believes his wife needs to stand up for herself more. Instead of giving her unsolicited advice about how to be more assertive, he could simply *be assertive*. He could demonstrate assertiveness in situations she's around to witness. He could also share anecdotes of times when he stood up for himself and it proved effective in getting what he wanted. By doing this Patrick would be, in essence, adding assertiveness into the relationship.

This works better than giving advice in myriad ways. First off, through the process of relating, Cynthia and Patrick have established that she can see his traits in her and he can see her traits in him. Relating makes their traits feel fluid. Once she notices that he has a trait that would serve her well, she naturally adopts it. And possibly best of all, she'll feel as though she made the decision all on her own to start being more assertive.

In other words, modeling *works better* than giving advice because it makes the other person more likely to make the change you'd like to see. Moreover, it doesn't just tell her to be different. It *shows her how* to be different. Advice is telling; modeling is showing.

The fact that modeling really works has been known for decades and has been tested in many different areas of science. Modeling is something we are biologically inclined to do. It's well known that people who like each other tend to mimic each other's actions — but this is not simple copying. It's not even a conscious choice.

Rather, it happens on a *cellular* level. The cells responsible for our unconscious modeling are called *mirror neurons*. Mirror neurons live in the motor cortex of the brain and become activated when another person is performing an action we relate to. That action is experienced in our brains as if *we are performing the action ourselves*.

As reported in *Scientific American*:

In the early 1990s, a team of neuroscientists at the University of Parma made a surprising discovery: Certain groups of neurons in the brains of macaque monkeys fired not only when a monkey performed an action — grabbing an apple out of a box, for instance — but also when the monkey watched someone else performing that action; and even when the monkey heard someone performing the action in another room. In short, even though these "mirror neurons" were part of the brain's motor system, they seemed to be correlated not with specific movements, but with specific goals.

So what does that mean for us? It means modeling is a way of *setting an unconscious goal* for your partner. He'll see you achieving something and will feel naturally compelled to achieve the same thing.

Modeling is a stellar method for evoking change. And just as important, it will not create distance between the two of you. It's the best way to influence another person without making him resistant, without challenging his autonomy, without coming from a place of superiority... and all the while communicating caring.

What the Relationship Gets You

We understand why it's a good idea to *create* a relationship with your partner: it allows the relationship to be extremely close without challenging either person's individual identity. The relationship is a representative that functions as the two of you united together, but *is not actually either of you.*

But what does the relationship-as-separate-entity actually do for you? What does it get you?

First, it gets you more closeness without your having to sacrifice personal independence. Each person in the relationship can still have his or her individual needs and values. These needs and values can be developed and honored separately from the other person's needs and values. Differences pose no threat. In other words, the relationship-as-separate-entity gets you freedom. Freedom and closeness *can* coexist. The relationship makes it possible.

The relationship (as discrete from either individual) also

fulfills the desire to be and act as one. It removes the pressure to fuse your individual selves together — each person losing some of him- or herself in the process.

Bountiful research shows that trying to fuse yourselves together is a really bad idea. It's sometimes described as having no personal boundaries or as being codependent, and it does have consequences. At best, one person will likely try to pull away, as discussed earlier. At worst, it can do lasting psychological harm.

As social psychologists Debra J. Mashek and Michelle D. Sherman wrote, "We propose that desiring less closeness with someone, or feeling 'too close,' means feeling that another person's influence (or even demands) on the self is too strong or intense, overpowering, unwelcome, or misguided.... In fact, we propose that this connection is a causal one: that perceived threat to personal control is one *cause* of feeling too close."

In other words, closeness done wrong can result in a loss of personal control. And even if you really wanted to lose yourself in another person, the result would never be a fair, equal melding. Equality can't really survive in that arrangement. One partner's personality and goals would inevitably take over, and the other person would start to disappear. This is the dark side of getting close. It can and should be avoided at all costs.

The relationship is the place where complete melding, complete fusing, can happen — fulfilling the legitimate desire to be united with a close partner — while you both still remain yourselves. You're both still your own people *and* you're both "one" in the context of the relationship.

The relationship is where you two are really in it together. If one of you has a great day at work, the relationship is filled with great feelings — giving you both access to those great feelings.

If one of you has lost a job, the relationship reflects that loss. The unity, yet discreteness, of the relationship makes this possible.

Both of you can take credit for the successes of the relationship, and you both have to take responsibility for its failures. You can both feel pride when one of you succeeds (as opposed to the competitiveness and jealousy that come from complete and total separateness), because the success is written into the shared document that you both get credit for.

Making a relationship is one of the fundamental underpinnings of caring. I am still me and you are still you, but we care enough to create something together. The two of you are now unified in a common purpose: making the relationship as full of caring as possible. Your interests are aligned. You can shoot for as much closeness as humanly possible.

Questions for Reflection

- Have you ever been "too close" to another person? What was that relationship like? How did it play out?
- Is there anyone you often find yourself mirroring? What qualities does that person have that you'd like to have more of in yourself?
- How do you typically react when someone gives you unsolicited advice?

 An Exercise to Challenge Yourself

If you're currently in a relationship (a romantic one in particular), make a list of everything special about your relationship — just as my husband and I did for our wedding. Include memories, inside jokes, references, and so on. This process will give you a great perspective on what making a relationship is all about!

Chapter Summary

- When it comes to closeness, *relationship* has a very specific definition: it is an entity that exists separate from either person but that contains everything the people involved share. The relationship is a representative that functions as the two of you united, but *is not actually either of you.*

- This way of thinking matters because highly caring relationships run the risk of challenging our identity and autonomy. So remember: a relationship is a separate entity from either of you. It is something the two of you create; it is not a new identity.

- There are two absolutely essential orientations for a long-lasting, deeply caring, and satisfying relationship: relating and equality. Relating means being able to see your humanity in someone else, through the reciprocal act of sharing human experiences. Equality means that you do not approach your partner from a place of superiority.

- To influence your partner without taking away her personal control, try modeling the behavior you'd like to see in her. Modeling is more likely to give you the results you want and is much less likely to create distance between the two of you.

Chapter 12

Showing Another Person You Care

In January 2015 a spunky little app called Invisible Boyfriend debuted in the mobile app store. "You're going to hate it," my friend Lindsay warned me. "I am? What's it about?" I wondered.

In its own words, Invisible Boyfriend "gives you real-world and social proof that you're in a relationship — even if you're not — so you can get back to living life on your own terms." For just $25 a month, your Invisible Boyfriend — who's actually an assortment of real people, not a robot — will text and call you just like a real boyfriend would.

"No way; I love it!" I told Lindsay.

"You do?" she cried.

"Yep. People are totally going to fall in love with these boyfriends!"

And indeed they have. In a *Washington Post* article titled "I Paid $25 for an Invisible Boyfriend, and I Think I Might Be in Love," Caitlin Dewey explains that despite her awareness that "one of the core premises of Invisible Boyfriend...is that the user will not, under any circumstance, fall in love with her fictional beau" she admits it's kind of hard not to.

He checks in with her every morning. He wants to know how

she's doing. He responds with concern and support when something bad happens. He gets ecstatic when something great happens. He's interested. He cares.

Sound ridiculous? It kind of is. But one thing it's *not* is mysterious. It isn't actually love these women are feeling... it's closeness. When I said closeness can be created with anyone, I really meant it!

The thing that Invisible Boyfriend is getting right is *showing care*. The Invisible Boyfriend expresses care for the "girlfriend" on the other end — in small, subtle, sustained moments of interest and affection. It's the check-ins, the "just wanted to see how you're doing today's." It's the spontaneous "thinking of you's" and the unprovoked smiles.

When we think about showing someone we care, this isn't usually what we envision. Instead, we think of grand gestures. We think of the extravagant birthday present, the Valentine's Day dinner, the annual girls-only or guys-only trip. In a business setting, we think of showing care as giving praise or granting a promotion.

While grand gestures are awesome (who doesn't like them?) and certainly should be part of your caring repertoire, the occasional grand gesture will not generate enough closeness to make up for day-to-day interactions that lack caring. It's the small moments that are the real substance of showing another person you care.

In other words, it's almost impossible to consistently omit the message "I really care about you" from your actions and then expect one grand gesture to make up for it. Think of the distant family member who makes the effort to send you a small gift every Christmas. You may very well appreciate the gesture and think it's sweet. But does it make you feel close to him? Probably not.

Caring must be shown all the time; ideally, caring should be shown every time you interact with your partner. But don't panic! Showing you care will, with enough practice, become so natural you'll hardly know you're doing it.

To learn the skill of showing someone you care, we'll begin with a shift in your thinking. I ask that you let go of the idea that you can create a close, lasting relationship based on a handful of nice gestures. I ask that you stop storing up your caring for a rainy day. Stop thinking big — and think small!

How to Be Engaged

The key to creating caring in every interaction with a friend, family member, love interest, or business associate is actually quite simple: be engaged. Being engaged, as I define it, has two components:

1. **Being present:** being both physically and mentally present with your partner (not texting excessively or getting lost in the memory of what happened at work earlier that day).
2. **Demonstrating interest:** responding with interest to his attempts to engage with you. This takes physically being together to the level of *being together*...emotionally and mentally. This makes an interaction *feel close*.

Being present and demonstrating interest — collectively defined as being engaged — are the acts that communicate caring in normal, day-to-day interactions. If you have these qualities in your interactions, it matters much less what the topic of conversation is or what activity you're doing together. These acts transform any interaction — mundane or thrilling — into an opportunity to create closeness. They act as an endless series of tiny, almost imperceptible, moments of support, affection, and kindness.

These regular moments of support, affection, and kindness are just as important as being there for your partner during a crisis. Of course, you still *should* be there for her during a crisis, but waiting for a crisis in order to communicate caring is a bit foolish. It also creates an awkward dynamic in which you start seeing a tragedy in another person's life as an opportunity for you to show how nice you can be.

Don't just show up when things are bad. Show up when things are great, good, fine, and okay. Taken all together, these moments create unlimited opportunities to communicate caring and create closeness.

Let's look at day-to-day engagement in action. Let's say your roommate — whom you want to be close to — is playing around on his computer and finds a funny cat video. He pulls you over to watch it with him. Which of the following do you do?

A. Watch and giggle with him. The cat is so fluffy.
B. Get up and leave him to watch it himself. "That's cool, but I've got stuff to do."
C. Tell him that he needs to stop wasting his time on cat videos.

Only response A is an engaged response. Responses B and C will make your roommate feel some level of disengagement. Depending on how sensitive he is to these types of subtle rejections, this one moment of not being engaged may make him retreat a little. But just a little retreating, over a long period of time, equals a lot of loneliness.

Let's take a closer look at responses B and C. It's pretty obvious why response C would make your roommate feel rejected: it's criticizing him as a person and categorizing his attempt to have a fun moment with you as "wasting time." It's also pretty close to being hostile.

The problems with response B are much subtler. It wouldn't

be wrong to call response B objectively neutral. But it's also a response that evokes the feeling of rejection. Why? Because every time your roommate wants to share his world with you, and you're not interested, he gets a little closer to believing you're not interested *in him*. And showing disinterest in him is the same thing, on an emotional level, as saying you don't care about him.

That is essentially all there is to being engaged in a way that communicates caring in everyday interactions. Show up, be present, be kind. Sounds pretty simple, right? So what makes it so hard to actually *do* this?

The first thing that often interrupts this flow of engagement is simple impulse control. All people struggle with impulse control to varying degrees, but for some people, the urge to snap at the first moment of feeling annoyed or frustrated is a real challenge. It *is* legitimately difficult to smile and laugh at a cat video if your roommate didn't do the dishes last night like he promised to.

The thing to do when you're legitimately frustrated or annoyed with someone you want to be close to — but know it's really best to stay engaged — is to separate the person from the problem as best you can. Transform the situation in your mind to: I care about my roommate, and the dishes need to be done. Both things can be true at the same time.

The goal to keep in mind, in this frustrating moment, is to believe — because it's true — that your roommate is way more likely to go do the dishes right away if you remind him he promised to do them *after* you've successfully communicated caring through being engaged. In the same way modeling isn't just nicer but actually *works better* than giving advice, staying engaged when you're frustrated isn't just nicer; it makes your partner *way* more likely to want to please you.

The other way in which we derail engagement is by denying ourselves a moment when we really need one. Let's say, when you got home from work, it wasn't the dirty dishes that got in your head, but the fact that one of your best friends at work got fired that day. You may genuinely need to process this event before you can watch a silly video and laugh, and that's perfectly legitimate. Your job in this situation is to ask your roommate for a moment.

Remember the principle of reciprocity in relationships: "I give you your moment, and you give me my moment." If your partner is committed to this principle, he'll certainly table his YouTube watching to give you your moment — if he knows you need one.

I once coached a couple — we'll call them Jessa and Lena — who had reached out to me because they were concerned they no longer had much in common. Jessa expressed that she felt very disconnected from Lena. She worried they were growing apart.

When we met in person, it was quite clear to me that Lena was indeed disengaged. She often stared off, even when Jessa was expressing raw emotion. She appeared to not really be listening. To me, she seemed utterly distracted.

"Jessa, what does rejection look like to you?" I asked.

"Well, for example," she began, "I started a new job last week and so far I love it. But Lena hasn't asked me a single thing about it. She really seems like she couldn't care less."

Lena's face collapsed in a frown. "That's not true...I definitely do care. I'm really happy you found something you love. I've just got a lot going on."

"Like what?" Jessa retorted.

"I didn't want to tell you this," Lena began, "but I think my mom is really sick. She's trying to act like she's not, but something's definitely wrong with her."

Jessa's eyes widened. "Why didn't you tell me that?"

"You were so happy about the new job...I didn't want to bring you down," Lena confessed.

What happened here? Lena had a legitimate reason to "need a moment" — she was worried about her mom's health. But because she didn't ask for a moment (or perhaps didn't really understand that she needed one), she gave the impression of not caring about a special moment in her partner's life. As good as her intentions were — not wanting to bring Jessa down — her actions did not communicate caring. Sometimes the most caring thing you can do is allow yourself to be cared for.

Lena and Jessa's story also illustrates the importance of being engaged when your partner is struggling with something significant. This form of engagement is usually called "support" and is critical in relationships. But support is not riding in on a white horse...it's not swooping in to save the day. It's not even trying to fix the problem. In Lena and Jessa's case, Jessa couldn't have fixed the problem of Lena's mom's health even if she tried.

So what does it really mean to support someone?

It turns out that support is defined by its level of engagement. In a study led by psychologist Natalya C. Maisel, sixty-seven couples were asked to report whether they had discussed a difficulty outside the relationship with their partner that day. The results indicated that both "visible" support (support that the provider reported providing and that the recipient reported receiving) and "invisible" support (support that the provider reported providing but the recipient did not report receiving) only reduced stress if the support demonstrated presence and interest.

In other words, the *fundamental nature* of support is engagement. It's being there for someone in the truest sense.

How to Fight Right

Engagement is the goal when things are great, good, fine, okay, and even when things are sad. But what about when things get heated? Is it possible to communicate caring when you and another person are having a conflict?

The answer is absolutely yes. But that doesn't mean it's particularly easy. It's very common for your awareness that you care about the other person's well-being to go out the window once you start feeling angry or attacked. But this is a moment when communicating caring — even in the midst of a fight — really matters.

Plainly put, it's perfectly possible to disagree with someone and still care about her.

Disagreements cannot — and should not — be avoided in close relationships. As long as disagreements don't devolve into physical fights, abusive, domineering, or intimidating behaviors, conflict can be a productive aspect of a relationship.

Conflicts are an opportunity for the relationship to grow. Much like complaining, as discussed earlier, conflict is a finger pointing at something and saying, "I care about this!" In this case, it's a finger pointing at an aspect of the relationship that could be better. Conflict is positive change, trapped.

The way to unleash the power of positive change that's trapped in conflict is to "fight right." Fighting right is a process in which both people express their perspectives effectively but also communicate caring. This process has to hit certain notes to work. To illustrate these important points, I've broken down fighting right into three distinct phases.

As you'd expect, these phases usually do not go in smooth order. It's perfectly fine to jump around among the phases, to start one phase, take a break, and then come back to it later. But it's crucial that each phase get touched on during the fight. If not, the fight has little chance of producing positive change and will likely create more distance in your relationship.

Fight Phase 1

The first phase of fighting should be wholly about you. The fight starts before you ever say a word to the other person. The fight starts when you start feeling the hard emotions that generally spark conflicts — anger, jealousy, frustration, annoyance.

When you get good at being with and identifying your own emotions, it's ideal to investigate your hard emotions to find the soft ones that lie beneath them before the fight even starts. Remember what we discussed in "Feeling the Power of Feelings"? Challenge your hard emotions. Ask yourself, "What are they really about?" If you can excavate the soft emotion before saying anything harsh to your partner, many would-be fights will neutralize before they even start.

But, of course, we're only human. And for many of us, the ability to neutralize fights before they happen is out of reach. The real point of phase 1 — which I believe everyone can do if willing to practice — is to start with yourself.

Get your perspective straight. What *specific* parts of the situation are bothering you? It's a lot to ask not to barrel into the other person when you're upset, but you'll be so much better heard (and you'll say many more relevant things) if you've clarified what you're really upset about before confronting him or her. It's okay to not know everything you're feeling and everything you want to say...but know *something*.

Phase 1 is also the time to get your physiology straight. Fighting with someone you care about is a situation in which you're extremely primed to get hijacked by your amygdala. It's very likely your feeling brain will perceive a potential fight as a threat and will recruit the rest of the brain. And as we know, this precludes us from thinking. If at all possible, don't go into a fight when you're literally not able to think.

Phase 1 is the ideal place to start, but what if your partner ignites the fight before you get a chance to get your thoughts and feelings straight? What if she skips doing her own phase 1 and starts throwing jabs?

This is not a pleasant experience for anyone, and physiological self-soothing is going to be essential in this moment. Try to soothe yourself with the knowledge that just because the first moments of the fight are hostile does not mean the fight is now inherently out of control. Don't throw away an attempt to fight right just because your partner set the tone poorly. The fight can absolutely be salvaged.

It's well known in the field of conflict management that the course of a conflict is not determined by the person who initiates the conflict but by the person who responds. In other words, your partner may say something explosive, but it's how you respond that determines whether any further bombs will be detonated.

So, even if you're getting attacked, help yourself get physiologically calm enough to be able to think. Once you can think, help your partner through her own phase 1. Help her clarify what she's feeling, and identify what *specifically* is making her upset. Use the exploration and investigative skills you learned so far. If she isn't skilled at starting with herself yet, remind her.

Helping her in this moment is not an act of charity; it absolutely benefits you too. If you help her through her own phase 1, she'll be more likely to do it on her own next time. Helping her with this benefits the whole relationship.

Fight Phase 2

Phase 2 is where the two of you communicate what's bothering you. There's no script for this part — no set of things to say and not say during a fight. And most everyone finds communicating clearly during a fight difficult.

I've found that the thing to use as your anchor during phase 2 is the knowledge that your partner is fully human. Humanizing the person — going soft on the person — will help both of you disentangle the people from the problem, allowing you to speak about the problem more easily, and to eventually start resolving it.

Do keep in mind all that we've learned about what types of language work and don't work for creating closeness. Rephrase if you find yourself going into interrogating ("why") or accusatory ("you") language. When the other person is speaking, use the listening techniques you learned in the knowing chapters (restating, reframing, etc.). Focus on better understanding his perspective — you'll not lose your own perspective by understanding his!

When you speak, remember to speak from your own perspective and not to attempt to "tell your partner the truth." You don't hold the truth any more than he does. Speak from your "I" and allow him to speak from his "I." Both are valid, and both need to be heard before the conflict can be resolved.

Notice your partner's emotions, and try to empathize during this phase. Pay special attention to any soft emotions that arise. These soft emotions will eventually pull you both out of the fight. When you have both tapped into some soft emotion and each understand the other person's perspective well enough to state his perspective to his satisfaction, you're ready to move out of phase 2.

Before we leave phase 2, there's one thing I want to make very clear. Just because you're going soft on the person doesn't mean you should *be soft* — that is, weak or compliant. It's vital to the long-term health of the relationship that your perspective be heard and that your feelings be acknowledged. Your needs, values, feelings, and thoughts are just as valid as his. Don't conceal or disavow these just to get the fight "over with."

Psychologist Dan Wile beautifully captures the importance of owning one's feelings during a conflict in his book *After the*

Fight. In this book he details the array of problems that can arise from not feeling entitled to one's own feelings:

> We feel sad and think we should not feel sad (we feel unentitled to our sadness). We tell ourselves: "Being sad doesn't help. I shouldn't let things get to me the way I do. I should be able to look on the positive side. And, anyway, I should be over it by now."
>
> We feel angry, and we think we should not feel angry (we feel unentitled to our anger) because we feel we have insufficient justification for it; thus we suppress it. But then, some time later, we blurt it out in a more eruptive and provocative form than if we had expressed the anger directly in the first place. Feeling unentitled to a feeling (in this case, anger) has produced a problem.

What Wile is saying here is that although it's undoubtedly uncomfortable, being straightforwardly sad or straightforwardly angry will ultimately bring the two of you closer than denying your feelings will. Be courageous when communicating your truth. Be brave in the fight! You are recognizing your partner's humanity, to be sure, but you're defending your own humanity as well.

Fight Phase 3

In phase 3 you and your partner start wrapping up the fight. This entails shifting the "I-ness" of phase 2 to a new "we-ness." This is when you invoke your relationship-as-separate-entity. This is the time when you come together, united in the place of "we."

Once you're both in the mind frame of we, search your individual perspectives for places of agreement. What were some things you said in common? No matter how volatile the fight, there will always be some places where you can agree. And even a small agreement is a place to start from.

Try not to fall into the trap of believing that "if we agree on something, that thing isn't part of what we're fighting about." The fight isn't just about the contentious points — it's about *all the points*. In other words, anything you said during phase 2 is part of the fight. There will be more-contentious points and less-contentious points. The less-contentious points will be part of the solution.

Now we're ready to end the fight — to come to a resolution. A resolution has two aspects.

The first aspect is "solving the problem." Remember what we learned earlier? Once you both see the problem as something separate from either of you, you can work together as a team to find a solution. This is the time to do just that. This is the time to get creative. Brainstorm as many ideas as you can think of to annihilate the problem.

The second — and much less understood — aspect of coming to a resolution is being able to talk about the problem going forward. Realistically, most problems don't have simple solutions and, even if you do hit on a perfect solution during your brainstorming, it'll likely take some time to execute. You'll probably need to have some ongoing discussions about the problem and solution — and you don't want these future discussions to reactivate the fight.

You've likely heard it said that it's a bad sign for a relationship if you are having the same fight over and over again. If you find yourselves in this situation, it's probably because you've never touched on this second aspect of complete resolution.

At the end of a fight, it's ideal to reduce the stress of the conflict by having a calm moment of bonding. If it's a relationship where you touch, get physically close — cuddle, hold hands, hug. If it's a platonic or professional relationship, use humor and lightness to bring both partners' physiologies back to rest.

This is a model for a complete, ideal fight, from beginning to end. It's a good way to fight while still communicating caring.

Why "If" Doesn't Work

One aspect of fighting that deserves special attention is apologizing. Once a fight is in full throttle, apologizing is the fastest way to deescalate heated emotions and get back on a path to resolution. Apologizing well is an excellent way to create closeness.

In essence, apologizing means that you take responsibility for a least a portion of the situation that upset the other person or that escalated the fight. While I wouldn't recommend apologizing for the whole fight — it's never just one person's fault — admitting that you did at least one thing wrong or made one mistake can quickly neutralize a conflict. It also instantly compels your partner (if she relates to you and can see herself in you) to think of things she may want to apologize for herself.

So how does one apologize well?

Let's start with the words some people dread: "I'm sorry." You certainly *can* apologize without saying these words…but you shouldn't.

Anything other than "I'm sorry" can be interpreted as a fake apology. Saying "I'm sorry" sincerely (not sarcastically or contemptuously) is the only way to make absolutely certain your partner knows you're apologizing. It'll be harder for her to continue being heated about something that she *knows for sure* you just apologized for.

Once you've committed to saying "I'm sorry," you'll need to be specific about what you're sorry for. This is where most well-intentioned apologies fall apart. Specificity is essential. And above all, don't use the word *if.*

For example, "I'm sorry if I hurt your feelings" is, plain and simple, not a real apology. "I'm sorry if you felt that way." "I'm sorry if you misunderstood what I'm saying." Placing "if" in your apology negates the whole thing because the point of apologizing in the first place is to take some responsibility. "If" puts the responsibility back on the other person. "I'm sorry if *you* felt that way." See that big glaring "you" there?

To apologize effectively, start with "I'm sorry I..." or "I'm sorry for..." and finish with something you yourself did that you know didn't help the situation. Be specific — this shows that you truly understand what you're taking responsibility for.

"I'm sorry if you felt that way" could become "I'm sorry I didn't call you back. I understand that hurt your feelings" or "I'm sorry for not letting you speak. I know that doesn't help." If you can't think of anything eloquent, simply say, "I'm sorry I hurt your feelings." That phrase, said with genuine sincerity, has the potential to quash a fight in an instant. Not to mention the fact that it's one of the simplest and most powerful ways to communicate caring.

Questions for Reflection

- In what ways could you be more engaged with other people? What's getting in the way of being engaged with others?
- How do you usually act when you know you need a moment to yourself? Do you ask for that moment? Do you silently withdraw? Do you pick a fight?
- Is there anything in any of your relationships you'd like to take responsibility for? Are you willing to apologize for it (without using "if," of course!)?

An Exercise to Challenge Yourself

The next time you find yourself about to have a disagreement with another person, focus on having a "perfect fight." Perform all three phases of fighting right as best you can, and help the other person through his or her phases as well. Notice how the fight feels different, and pay attention to the phases that were most challenging for you.

Chapter Summary

- The occasional grand gestures won't generate enough closeness to make up for day-to-day interactions that do not communicate caring. Caring must be shown all the time; ideally, caring should be shown every time you interact with your partner.

- You accomplish this by staying engaged. Being engaged, as I define it, has two components:

    1. Being present with your partner both physically and emotionally.

    2. Demonstrating interest by responding to her attempts to engage you.

- Engagement is the goal when things between the two of you are calm. But when things get heated, the goal becomes to "fight right." The way to fight without creating distance is to hit certain notes. Ideally every fight touches on these three phases:

    1. Start with yourself. Get your perspective and your physiology straight.

    2. Communicate your perspective.

3. Shift from communicating your individual perspectives to joining as a team to resolve the problem together. In addition to solving the problem, agree that it's okay to continue talking about the problem going forward. This will prevent the two of you from having the same fight over and over again.

Part 4

Mastering
the Art of
Closeness

Chapter 13

Creating a Culture of Closeness

Have you ever noticed that once you achieve something you've always wanted, it's hard to feel sustained pleasure in having it? Once you purchase your dream home, you want to repaint it. Once you repaint it, you want new furniture. Once you attain something you've longed for, you can't long for it anymore.

This phenomenon, discussed in the three-part PBS documentary *This Emotional Life*, is called "hedonic adaption." It is described as "our tendency to quickly adapt to our changing circumstances. This is why people who win the lottery, for instance, usually find themselves at the same level of happiness they had before they won."

But not always: "Close relationships, however, may be an exception. In contrast to material goods, we are more likely to continue to want our close relationships, even after we attain them, and to continue to derive positive emotions from them."

It turns out that feeling known and cared about never gets old. Feeling less alone never goes out of style. Closeness is one strategy for attaining lifelong, consistent happiness.

So how do we go about maintaining and sustaining closeness

in all our relationships, given that circumstances change, relationships change, and people change? Is it inevitable that just because disagreements and difficulties will arise, distance will arise? Is there a strategy for maintaining lifelong closeness?

There is! I call it creating a culture of closeness.

A culture of closeness is something you and another person actively create together, just like closeness itself. It acts as a framework — a structure of mutually understood references — around which your closeness can grow. It's a way of seeding into the relationship reminders that the two of you know each other well and care about each other deeply. In this way, a culture of closeness makes your relationship firm and resilient.

A culture of closeness also streamlines the process of continuing to know and care about each other over long periods of time. It essentially transports you both from having to actively work at knowing and caring — all the efforts we've discussed so far — to having attained unconscious competence at knowing and caring. When you create a culture of closeness, you graduate from learning about what makes people feel close to one another to being experts at your relationship.

So what exactly does a culture of closeness mean? We know what closeness means: access to another person's inner world through the acts of knowing and caring. What's a "culture"?

Merriam-Webster's Dictionary defines the word *culture* as the "beliefs, customs, arts, etc., of a particular society, group, place, or time." A more specific definition comes from the social science literature: "Rather than membership in monolithic groups, we instead define culture as explicit and implicit patterns of historically derived and selected ideas and their embodiment in institutions, practices, and artifacts."

Both these definitions are useful to reflect on. But for our purposes, I define *culture* as a system of patterns that reflects your closeness back to you. It's a set of deliberate reminders — reminders that the two of you know each other well and care about each other deeply. You create this culture together because you're connected through common language, common purpose, and a common goal: the survival of your mutual closeness.

The culture the two of you create will be highly personalized and customized to your relationship. It'll end up being however the two of you want it to be. That's part of the joy of a culture of closeness. That's part of the fun!

But there are some aspects of culture that all highly developed and long-lasting relationships touch on, at least a little:

- Shared meaning systems
- Shared memories and experiences
- Shared purpose
- Gifting

Let's learn more about what these categories entail. And remember: knowing and caring are never done. The culture you create simply enhances, streamlines, and reinforces your efforts.

Shared Meaning Systems

The first way to create a culture of closeness is to establish shared meaning systems. A shared meaning system is a set of ways in which a group of people *make something mean something*. This may sound odd, but it's something we do all the time without being aware of it. When you walk into a jewelry store and look around, it's all just jewelry — until you pick out a necklace, buy it, give it to your friend on her birthday, and notice that she wears it every time the two of you hang out together. Through the thought and effort you put into getting it for your friend, you made the necklace mean something. You both now recognize it as a symbol that means "we are friends."

There are innumerable ways of creating meaning with someone. When you and your boyfriend develop a favorite brunch routine, you've made the meal mean something. When you and your coworker high-five every time you make a sale, you've made the act mean something. When you and your dad re-create your favorite pretzel recipe from your childhood, you've made a baked good mean something.

It sounds so easy, right? In many ways, shared meaning systems *are* very easy to establish. Pick a reference — something you both like, something you both remember — and institutionalize it by doing it *with intention*.

It's the intention part that we usually leave out. We may go to brunch with our boyfriend all the time but remain unaware that we've imbued the meal with meaning. This is what I encourage you to focus on when establishing shared meaning systems: do it intentionally. Don't fall into habits and patterns with your partner just *because*. Habits can just as easily foster distance as they can closeness. Consciously choose the best aspects of your relationship — the closest, the most fun, the most inspiring parts — and make them a central part of your culture.

There are several ways to *make something mean something*, including:

- **Customs/attitudes:** Customs and attitudes are beliefs you both share. They are mental orientations, like shared perspectives. You both believe it's appropriate to do business with family members or you both believe you can be spiritual without having any religious affiliation.
- **Rituals/routines:** Rituals and routines are regularly scheduled actions that have some deeper meaning. You and your cousin go to the gym together every morning because you both value health. Health is part of the culture

you've created together, and going to the gym is the ritual that reminds you of that.

- **Language/humor:** Altering language to reflect your relationship style lets you develop a closeness vocabulary all your own. Humor, especially inside jokes, brings your particular brand of playfulness to your culture. If both your names start with *K* change words that start with *C* to start with *K*. Every time you see a *K* you'll be reminded of your kulture of kloseness!

- **Symbols/objects:** Symbols and objects are visual representations of your relationship. If you share a home, you can display these objects around the house. Some examples are pictures of the two of you, souvenirs from your travels together, and birthday or anniversary gifts.

In romantic relationships, the most common meaning option is usually objects. Displaying objects of significance in the home is so common for married couples, it's even been studied.

As social psychologist Ximena B. Arriaga reports, home objects "cue relationship qualities to the couple themselves.... Following this reasoning, we suggest that prominently placed home objects provide environment-specific ways of directing a couple member's thoughts, feelings, and actions. Just as there are ways of arranging items to informationally cue behaviors, there are ways that couple members may arrange the physical environment of their home to cue their couple identity."

So, if you live together, prominently displaying symbols and objects is a great way to start making shared meaning. In business relationships — in which members of the group usually don't live together — I suggest starting with rituals and routines. Regular, periodic meetings, social gatherings, and simple rituals (like the high-five example) will spring up organically. Notice when this is happening, harness it, and make it part of the group's culture.

Below are some ideas for creating shared meaning with the important people in your life. These are just suggestions — take them and make them your own.

Ideas for Love Relationships

- **Ritual:** At the end of every workday, get physically close and share the best and worst thing that happened that day. This is a great way to reinforce the fact that you know each other well.
- **Language:** Give yourself a "couple name" (like celebrities have). You could even think of it as the relationship-as-separate-entity's name.
- **Symbol:** One of the most recognizable couple symbols is the engagement or wedding ring. Customize these rings in ways that feel special and meaningful to you. You could, for example, engrave the band with some text that reminds you of your relationship, so that every time you look down at it you will remember your culture of closeness.

Ideas for Relationships with Family and Friends

- **Ritual:** Invent your own holiday. With a friend, start the tradition of celebrating your "friendiversary." With family, get everyone together for Thanksgiving in July or Easter in September.
- **Language:** Make the other person's trademark habits into verbs. With my friends, "arriving Kira-style" means being ten minutes early everywhere.
- **Symbol:** Display family and/or friend photos around your home. These are wonderful captured moments of your shared story through time.

Ideas for Business Relationships

- **Ritual:** At the end of the week, all team members gather and name one thing they did that week they're proud of, as well as one thing someone else did on the team that they appreciated.
- **Language:** Don't be afraid to use terminology or jargon from your industry — it's a great reminder of the context in which you met. For example, when a start-up changes its business focus, the term used is *pivoting*. Every time I see my old start-up friends, we playfully use this industry term to herald a change of any kind. "Oh, you're starting a new job next week? Pivot!"
- **Symbol:** Team logos! Wear clothing emblazoned with team or business logos to remind yourself that you're proud to be part of the team.

Making Memories

The second way in which two people create a culture of closeness is by making memories together. Memories are intrinsically tied to emotions, so the more the two of you are embedded in each other's memories, the more emotional access you will have to each other. In other words, doing memorable things together strengthens your emotional bond.

Of course, memories will be created over time in a long-term relationship whether you're meaning to make them or not. Why not consciously decide to make them as positive and special as possible? Making them special can mean doing something grand — taking your best friend on vacation or planning a surprise party — but it doesn't have to. Some of the most memorable moments are the smallest. Go explore a new neighborhood together, or have a conversation you've never had with anyone else.

Memories are exceptionally useful in creating a culture of closeness because they feed into every other aspect of your culture. Take shared meaning systems, for example. The reason displaying wedding photos around the house has an impact on a married couple is that both partners remember the feeling of making that commitment. The photo doesn't have power without the memory.

To be sure, making memories isn't about throwing down big bucks or sweeping the other person off his feet. Making memories is simply about being intentional. Put thought into what you're doing with your partner. Take note of what's around you when you're together. What does it look like? What does it smell like? Commit these sensations to memory. Be in the moment.

No discussion of making memories can be had without addressing the elephant in the room: your phone. We've all experienced being taken out of the moment by our ability to capture every nanosecond. While taking a handful of photos to look back on can certainly be in service of making memories, it can also easily distract from the experience. And it's the experience that matters.

Mathias Crawford, Stanford University researcher in human-computer interactions, summarized the impact our phones are having on our experiences:

> Every experience is being mediated and conceived around how it can be captured and augmented by our devices. No place is this more apparent than our meals, where every portion leading up to, during and after a dining experience is being carved out by particular apps.
>
> People make dinner reservations on OpenTable; check in on Foursquare when they arrive at the restaurant; take a picture of their food to share on Instagram; post on Twitter a joke they hear during the meal; review the restaurant on Yelp; then, finally, coordinate a ride home using Uber.

If you're wondering when people are going to reject the phone, that will mean they need to reject Silicon Valley's entire concept of how you ought to be dining.

Some of the ways in which we use our phones can certainly add to the experience of making memories with those we want to be close to. There's no need to leave your phone at home to have a good time. The trick is, when you're actively making memories, to use your phone to enhance the experience and not detract from it.

Here are some ideas for making memories together:

Ideas for Love Relationships

- Focus on moments that mark the passage of time: weddings, anniversaries, date-iversaries. These help you organize your memories to create a mental construct of your shared story.
- Do physically stimulating activities together such as biking, hiking, and rock climbing.
- Celebrate successes. Did your wife just retire, get promoted, or get accepted to grad school? Successes are already pretty memorable — use this opportunity to make them even more so!

Ideas for Relationships with Family and Friends

- Try out new hobbies together. Take a painting class or go wine tasting — make memories out of your shared interests.
- With family, making memories often involves food. Help out in the kitchen. If one of your relatives is usually in charge of making Thanksgiving dinner, jump in there and help. You will both remember those moments together for a long time to come.

- Plan a trip with your friend(s). Friends-only trips are amazing ways to make memories in your platonic relationships, and they don't have to be extravagant. Get everyone to sleep over at one friend's house on a Saturday night, and then go to brunch all together Sunday morning.

Ideas for Business Relationships

- Make time for team lunches or dinners. Get the team out of the office for something as simple as a meal; the change in environment will get everyone talking about new topics.
- Learn new skills together. Memory and learning are interrelated, so learning new skills together is an excellent way to make shared memories. It has the added benefit of making the team more proficient.
- Plan off-site trips. Take your team somewhere they don't normally go, even for an afternoon. It'll help stimulate conversation between team members who don't normally have a reason to talk to one another.

Shared Purpose

We usually think of our life purpose as the things we pursue to give life meaning, or as the actions we take to have a certain impact on the world. These purposes are highly personal, much like values. In fact, it wouldn't be wrong to say that life purposes are values put into action.

Because these are so personal, identifying purposes that you share with another person is a highly intimate and special thing to do. Infusing purpose into your relationship gives your culture of closeness great depth of meaning. While it is an advanced technique in creating and maintaining closeness, sharing purpose is not all that hard to do.

The starting point from which to share purpose with another person is to look at your individual values — the things you deeply care about. Which ones do you have in common? Which ones overlap? If you're creating a culture of closeness with someone, you likely know him very well and can easily identify values the two of you share.

If identifying shared values isn't so obvious, I recommend that you both (separately) list twenty of your values. Then share your lists with each other and notice where some of your values and some of his could be grouped together. Perhaps only one of you values "nature," but the other values "adventure." Those have enough overlapping qualities to be considered an opportunity to create shared purpose. Once you've identified your opportunities, pick a few to start working on.

Keep in mind that your values are the things you really care about...and that caring completely requires showing care. Pick a shared value and ask yourself how you could show that you care about this value. This may sound abstract, but it will lead you to some tangible things that the two of you can do together to promote your values in the world.

Let's say you and your sister both care very much about making sure children have good nutrition. You're both passionate about this topic and want to see real change happen. What are some ways you could put this mutual passion into action?

If one or both of you have children, you could exchange healthy recipes. You could get involved in the school lunch programs in your neighborhood. You could volunteer, make donations, or do some fund-raising together. Maybe you could coauthor a cookbook for children. Maybe it's as simple as encouraging each other to stay informed.

All these count as creating a shared purpose together. It matters very little how big or small the project is — from starting a business together to simply talking about the things you care about. All these activities infuse your relationship with purpose. In this way, you each have an impact on the world, and your relationship does too.

Here are some ideas to get you thinking about shared purpose opportunities:

- In love relationships, couples often create meaning and purpose together by starting a family. Having (or adopting) children and creating a home together can be a deep source of meaning and purpose for romantic couples.

- Family members and friends often find a shared purpose around community, social, and charitable projects. Perhaps a member of your family or a close friend suffered from an illness that you now find shared meaning and purpose in combating together.

- In business, shared values can be built right into a company's mission. For example, two partners in law could agree to devote a certain percentage of their resources to doing pro bono work. A value you and your business partner share can become at least part of what you want the business to achieve.

- Since you now both value closeness, promoting closeness in the world can always be one of the ways you create a shared purpose!

Gifting

In anthropology, a gifting culture is a culture in which gifts are exchanged by members of the group with no strings attached but with an understanding that the gifts will be reciprocated.

I see this same mind-set as one of the critical ways in which two people create a culture of closeness together. You give to your partner, not because you expect something in return, but because that is the culture the two of you have established. And because it is the culture, your partner will feel and act the same way — giving to you without expectation, just as you give to her.

When I use the word *gifts*, I mean it in the broadest sense possible. While physical gifts are wonderful and can be lovely symbols full of meaning, the foundation of your gifting culture is not tangible gifts. The foundation is *intangible* gifts — gifts of the heart — of which you have unlimited supply.

To name just a few:

- Appreciation
- Admiration
- Respect
- Freedom
- Nurture
- Space to evolve
- Encouragement
- Support
- Comfort
- Loving affection

These intangible gifts, given and received freely, round out your culture of closeness. The other culture categories — shared meaning systems, shared memories, and shared purpose — make your relationship sturdy and resilient. This one — shared gifting — makes your relationship tender and kind.

Ideas for Love Relationships

- "Just because" gifts. These can be the more traditional gifts — flowers, sweets, outings — but given at unpredictable moments. There's something absolutely endearing and memorable about receiving a "birthday gift" when it's not your birthday!

- "Date swaps." These are dates that one partner plans around the other partner's interests. Doing these regularly (switching back and forth between who's planning and who's receiving, of course) is like giving the gift of knowing. It says, "Not only do I know what you like but I'd like to give you opportunities to do more of it."
- Going "off-list." This means doing helpful things beyond your regular chore list without being asked to do them — doing the laundry even though you're not "expected" to do it. Not only is this very thoughtful, but it's giving the other person the gift of more free time.

Ideas for Relationships with Family and Friends

- Words of encouragement. Giving encouragement is an intangible gift that friends absolutely love receiving.
- The gift of play! If you know your friend could use a little hangout time without any heavy conversation, plan an outing in which talking is not the objective. Something active always works well — play tennis or organize a paintball game!
- The gift of being there. Families inevitably suffer a loss of one of their own or simply go through difficult times. Making yourself available — checking in, dropping by — can be the most precious gift during challenging times.

Ideas for Business Relationships

- The gift of feedback. There's a common saying in business management that "no feedback is the worst feedback." I take this to mean that sharing your experience of another person's work is a valuable gift. Just make sure you're presenting it as your experience of his or her work and not as the "truth."

- Advocating. Advocating for another person's contribution to the company is a very thoughtful gift. It can also have real consequences regarding his or her pay and promotions.

- Appreciation. Nowhere is appreciation more of a gift than in working environments. Feeling appreciated can make all the difference between feeling satisfied and disgruntled at work.

Questions for Reflection

- What is your favorite way of making meaning? Do you love symbols? Objects? Inside jokes?
- Whom do you know with values most similar to yours? Would she be open to sharing a purpose with you?
- What's one intangible gift that you'd like to receive from another? Are you willing to tell him about it?

 An Exercise to Challenge Yourself

Create a detailed description of your ideal culture of closeness with another person. Write down the answers to the following questions to better understand the personality of your culture:

- If your culture of closeness had a name, what would it be?
- If it were a person, what would it look like?
- If it had a voice, what would it sound like?
- What would it enjoy doing on the weekends?

Chapter Summary

- We maintain and sustain closeness with other people over the long term by creating a culture of closeness. A culture of closeness is a framework — a structure of mutually understood references — around which your closeness can grow. It's a way of seeding reminders of closeness into the relationship itself. This makes the relationship sturdy and resilient.

- Cultures of closeness are highly personalized and customized to your particular relationship. But they all touch at least a little on these aspects of culture:

  1. Shared meaning systems, also described as "making something mean something." These include rituals/ routines; customs/attitudes; language/humor; and symbols/objects.

  2. Shared memories and experiences. Memories are intrinsically tied to emotions, so the more the two of you are entwined in each other's memories, the more emotional access you have to each other.

  3. Shared purpose. Sharing a life purpose with another person is a highly intimate and special thing to do. Infusing purpose into your relationship gives your culture of closeness depth of meaning.

  4. Gifting. Give intangible gifts — the gift of appreciation, admiration, respect, encouragement, and loving affection just to name a few — not because you expect to receive something in return but because it's part of your mutual culture.

Chapter 14

Overcoming Obstacles at Work, at Home, and in Love

Although it's true that any relationship can be close and any relationship can be distant, each category of relationship (friend, family, spouse) faces its own specific set of challenges when it comes to creating closeness.

A relationship that starts at work will contain different preconceived notions about what's appropriate than one that springs from a family unit. In the former context, it may feel inappropriate to cry, while in the latter, crying is usually fine. A romantic relationship often has preconceived expectations — like an explicit commitment — that a friendship does not.

Many of these notions about *how certain relationships should be* set up obstacles to creating closeness. As we've learned, thinking that certain relationships should be a certain way is unhelpful because it's limiting. It reduces your opportunities to make yourself less lonely. To make yourself freer in your journey out of loneliness, you'll need to update and improve these limiting thoughts.

Let's look at the four major contexts in which people usually create closeness: at work, within their family, with their friends, and with romantic partners. What are the most common mental hurdles you'll encounter when trying to create closeness in each of these contexts?

The Three Big Mental Hurdles at Work

Mental Hurdle 1:

"Closeness sounds too intimate for work."

I wouldn't be surprised if you find it hard to imagine practicing closeness at work without crossing any professional boundaries. I've found, however, that coworkers can be professional and build closeness at the same time. Let's talk about how this works.

First of all, closeness is an entirely mutual interaction. If you ask someone at work a "needs and values" question and he doesn't want to answer, he's likely not the best candidate to attempt closeness with again. But the reality is that people at work are humans, and many of them feel very much the same way you do. If you feel drawn to someone at work and find yourself wanting to get lunch with her, she likely wants to get lunch with you too. Just ask!

Moreover, closeness — particularly caring, the most intimate aspect of closeness — really *benefits* working environments. Current studies show that the amount of caring expressed by coworkers in interactions outside the office (presumably when they feel freer to discuss more personal things) predicts how well they work together *within* the office.

In 2012 the *Harvard Business Review* published findings from a study conducted at MIT's Human Dynamics Laboratory that looked at a range of industries, including technology teams, hospitals, banks, and call centers to determine what made some teams perform better than others. The study gave participants electronic badges "that collected data on their individual communication behavior — tone of voice, body language, whom they talked to and how much, and more." The study found that "the best predictors of productivity were a team's energy and engagement outside formal meetings. Together those two factors explained one-third of the variations in dollar productivity among groups."

Remember what I said earlier when we discussed showing someone you care? "The key to creating caring in every interaction with a friend, family member, love interest, or business associate is actually quite simple: be engaged." I interpret the above study — which names "engagement" as a core component of team productivity — to be clear evidence for the productive power of caring...even at work. Closeness at work will certainly make you feel less lonely and it might even make your team work better together!

> **Mental Hurdle 1 reframed:** "Closeness doesn't have to cross any boundaries, and it can actually make teams function better."

Mental Hurdle 2:

"It's inappropriate to talk about feelings at work."

Keep in mind that feelings are not just yelling and crying. Feelings are an inherent part of any human group — including a group at work — and normalizing feelings in working environments actually reduces the likelihood of screaming matches or crying fits.

We all have feelings all the time, whether or not we acknowledge them. Someone working quietly may feel bored to tears, be seething with anger, be engrossed in the project at hand, or totally checked out. How do you know unless you ask?

So much information gets left on the table when feelings aren't allowed to be addressed at work. How you feel about your current project could be totally different from how you feel about your boss. How you feel about your team could be totally different from how you feel about your growth prospects at the company. Having knowledge of these nuances has obvious benefits for everyone involved.

You may be thinking, "Knowing how a coworker is feeling is one thing, but is it really appropriate to *show her* you care?" Of course! Caring simply means treating her as a full human, demonstrating interest in what happens to her, and being engaged when she reaches out to you. What could be inappropriate about that?

> **Mental Hurdle 2 reframed:** "Feelings are inextricable from people and from working environments. They are unavoidable, so let's work with them!"

Mental Hurdle 3:

"At work, sometimes people really are the problem."

There certainly are people in this world who are truly terrible to work with. Some are unqualified to do the job assigned to them. Some even take pleasure in causing problems — remember John Gottman's pit bulls and cobras? If you see red flags that indicate a truly disastrous personality — or find someone detestable for your own private reasons — it's perfectly fine to distance yourself.

But I see this as different from regularly considering other people as "problems." Is noticing that you deeply dislike your PR person and choosing to intentionally distance yourself from her the same as silently resenting her for sending out press releases full of typos? No. The first one is a conscious decision that serves you well; the second is conflating the person with the problem.

Because work projects are almost always collaborative — and the status of the whole group can rise and fall on one person's mistake — it's incredibly easy to conflate people with problems at work. We do this all the time.

The change in thinking I'd like you to make is this. Consider coworkers "innocent until proven guilty." Presume that your PR person is a decent human being who needs help resolving the problem of letting typos slip until you see evidence to the contrary. Assume that the problem is probably not caused by a character flaw in the person. You'll find that almost all the time, it's not.

> **Mental Hurdle 3 reframed:** "Let's give people the benefit of the doubt and assume the problem is separate from the person's character, until proven otherwise."

The Three Big Mental Hurdles in Families

Mental Hurdle 1:

> *"I grew up with you, so I already know you. What more is there to learn?"*

This mind-set is probably the single biggest stumbling block to closeness within families. It's a combination of complacency owing to the supposed permanence of family and the assumption of inherent knowledge of one another. As discussed earlier, no relationships are inherently closer than others, and this perspective is very detrimental to creating closeness within families.

How does one get past it? To start, cultivate curiosity. There's very likely *something* your brother or sister said recently that piqued your curiosity. There's likely *some* choice your cousin made recently that you don't fully understand. Give it a shot, and ask her about it. Remember to hold the most inviting mind-set you can and to pose well-crafted questions.

Another tip is to reflect on how much has changed since you were all kids. This can help you shake free of assuming your family members are the same as they were decades ago. You're not the same as you were ten, twenty, thirty years ago — why would anyone else in your family be either?

Mental Hurdle 1 reframed: "I can't assume I know your answer before I even ask you a question!"

Mental Hurdle 2:

"I can't be honest with my family — telling them too much just makes them worried, disappointed, or critical."

I find that family members very often create distance with one another because being honest and open seems scary. This is a complex topic, and there are whole books dedicated to helping families overcome this one hurdle: being open and honest with each other.

For our purposes here, keep one thing in mind: you don't need to create closeness with anyone who is not capable of creating closeness with you. If your father shows no signs of being able to accept new information about you, or your grown son never reciprocates your efforts to learn about him, or your sister cannot take responsibility for any part of your relationship — don't keep hurling yourself against that wall. Family members, just like anyone else, need to "pass the test" of being able to know and care.

To find individuals in your family you *can* potentially be close to, I recommend asking each a few deepening questions, just as you would with a stranger. When you do, look for the four characteristics of someone who is capable of knowing:

- Ability to self-disclose
- Ability to reciprocate moments
- Ability to accept new information
- Ability to be present

And the four characteristics of someone who is capable of caring:

- Ability to feel and express emotions
- Ability to respond appropriately
- Ability to take personal responsibility
- Ability to accept caring from others

Some families members may not pass the test, but others will. Those who do are your opportunities to create closeness within your family.

> **Mental Hurdle 2 reframed:** "Every family member is unique, and there may be one or two whom I can get close to."

Mental Hurdle 3:

"My family is not a family of equals. It's more like a hierarchy."

In some families, it's not assumed that everyone is an equal. Sometimes the parents are the parents and the children are the children, period, regardless of age. When this is the case — and the older generation doesn't feel comfortable sharing personal information or revealing vulnerabilities to the younger generation — it will be a challenge to have an extremely close relationship.

That being said, just because you may not be able to practice *every* closeness technique with a family member, and get very close in the process, doesn't mean you can't practice *any* of them. Your grandfather may never view you as an equal. You may never view him as fully human if he can't reveal any vulnerabilities. But that doesn't mean the two of you can't learn each other's stories. It doesn't mean you can't be engaged. It doesn't mean you can't show each other you care.

Closeness is not a zero-sum game. Some areas of personal life may be off-limits in some families, but others might be rich in opportunities to bring you closer.

> **Mental Hurdle 3 reframed:** "I might not be able to get really close to my family members, but a little closer is better than super distant."

The Three Big Mental Hurdles in Friendships

Mental Hurdle 1:

> *"I just want to have fun with my friends; I don't want to have heavy conversations all the time."*

Creating closeness with someone isn't all about having heavy conversations. Once you've established a good amount of knowing and caring, these efforts will be much less in the forefront of your mind — you'll be unconsciously competent at them and will hardly notice you're making them anymore.

That being said, having a few really intentional conversations — especially in the beginning — goes a long way toward getting close. They add a depth of satisfaction to a relationship that many people who struggle with loneliness crave. They are also highly effective for reducing loneliness and can be fun in and of themselves.

Moreover, these foundational conversations make the lighthearted times even more fun. If you know more about what your friend enjoys doing, you'll pick better activities to do together. If you've developed inside jokes, you'll laugh more. If you've learned how to engage, you'll be more engaged, no matter what you're doing together.

> **Mental Hurdle 1 reframed:** "A handful of meaningful conversations will make the fun times even more fun!"

Mental Hurdle 2:

> *"It's kind of weird to take friendships so seriously, especially new ones."*

For some people, friends are people with whom you enjoy doing casual activities — and that's about it. If this is as far as you want to take your friendships, and you don't battle loneliness, there's no reason to force these relationships any further.

That being said, there's also no reason why friendships can't be the most important relationships of your life. Ever seen *Sex and the City*, *Entourage*, *Golden Girls*, or... *Friends*? There are certain situations and stages of life in which friends are really the backbone of your social support system. There may be times when you don't want a romantic relationship. There may be times when you don't want to be drawn back into the family fold. These are the moments when friends can be everything.

Friendships have just as much potential to be meaningful and fulfilling as any other relationship. Try reframing the notion that "I'm taking my friendships too seriously" as "I'm being intentional about my relationships."

> **Mental Hurdle 2 reframed:** "I'm not being too serious; I'm being intentional about my relationships."

Mental Hurdle 3: .

> *"I've had the same friends forever. I don't feel like I can act any differently than I've always acted with them."*

In some ways it is indeed easier to create closeness with a new friend. Right from the beginning, you can establish the habits of actively knowing and caring. And if you find that the other person isn't really committed to putting in the effort, it's not much of a loss for you to disengage.

Existing friendships require that we *change* habits, which we all know can be a difficult feat. So before you go out on a limb and start initiating change, take a step back, and ask yourself a few simple questions. If you already have established friendships — and yet are struggling with loneliness — what's that about? What are you not getting from your friendships? What would you like to be different?

As you can see, the place to start tackling this hurdle is really with yourself. What are you craving? If it's more care, initiate some change in the way you and your friends show one another you care. If you feel as if your childhood friends don't know anything about you anymore, start with small acts of knowing. Start small, and see what a big difference the smallest changes can make.

> **Mental Hurdle 3 reframed:** "If I have friends but am feeling lonely, there's probably something lacking in my friendships. What might that thing be?"

The Three Big Mental Hurdles in Romance

Mental Hurdle 1:

> *"I don't want my husband or wife to create closeness with anyone but me."*

When you've made a commitment to be exclusive with someone, it's normal to feel as if you should have access to that person that others don't. I'd argue that you can indeed maintain special access to your spouse while letting him or her create closeness with others. It simply requires making a few distinctions.

First of all — as you're certainly aware — closeness is not sex. It doesn't *preclude* sex, but sexual intimacy is not a required ingredient in the closeness recipe. To put a finer point on it, closeness does not have to be flirty, suggestive, or romantic in any way. So in the realm of sexual exclusivity, closeness is no threat to an exclusive romantic relationship.

But what about the idea that becoming close to someone other than your spouse amounts to having an "emotional affair"? Here's where a second distinction comes into play: closeness is not love. The love the two of you share *is* unique and exclusive to the relationship. Your particular love really can't be re-created with anyone else, and I think the notion that "no one can understand the love we share" is true. Building closeness does not create, destroy, or redirect love. It's simply a way to reduce loneliness in your life.

> **Mental Hurdle 1 reframed:** "Closeness and love are different. Our love can be exclusive, while closeness is shared with many."

Mental Hurdle 2:

> "The relationship-as-separate-entity thing sounds really unromantic."

While viewing another person as your "other half" is indeed romantic, the reality is that if you think like this, the moment the other person does something you don't like or don't agree with, you'll take it as a personal affront. If your very notion of "yourself" is entangled with the other person, the stakes are so high — your very *self* is riding on it — that any small mistake on his or her part feels like a personal tragedy.

When this happens, the urge is typically either to pull away to protect your sense of self from being sullied or to attempt to change the other person into a "half" you want to be identified with. Both these routes are unfortunately slippery slopes back into loneliness.

If you can learn to let go of some outdated notions about romance, you'll find that the relationship-as-separate-entity is actually *more* romantic than fusing yourselves together. That's because it's a constant choice and a constant creation. Every day the two of you make the relationship together. You're creating something that's not you and not him...it's a new life in the world that the two of you make together.

Compare the dynamic action of making the relationship to the static state of just "being one person." Doesn't the latter sound a bit boring by comparison?

> **Mental Hurdle 2 reframed:** "The relationship-as-separate-entity is super romantic because it's an active, conscious creation."

Mental Hurdle 3:

> "I don't get how you can be married and have different values."

Problems do indeed arise in marriages when people have different values...and aren't aware of them. Major misunderstandings can occur when one spouse is acting in ways the other doesn't understand because the former isn't privy to the underlying source of the action. Remember Kim Kardashian's seventy-two-day marriage?

However, it's not really the value difference that causes these problems; it's the lack of awareness. Can a wife who values freedom and a husband who values nurturing have a great marriage? Absolutely! If they're aware of this difference, they can come up with a system that works for them. Maybe she gets all the space she wants until he wants her to nurture him, and then he asks for that. She nurtures him freely when he asks for it because she trusts he'll give her freedom again once he's feeling better.

However, if these two people remained unaware of their differences, he'd find her withholding or cold and she'd find him needy or clingy. Differences — even when they're deep ones — don't need to be chalked up to character flaws. Differences are not closeness killers, but lack of understanding of each other's inner worlds is. Once you understand what's motivating your spouse, that motivation can be integrated into the relationship.

> **Mental Hurdle 3 reframed:** "It's being unaware of each other's values that really causes problems."

These are the primary mental hurdles associated with each type of relationship, but they're certainly not the only ones. What reaction do *you* have when you think of creating closeness at work, in your family, in your friendships, and in your romantic relationship? Which of your ideas do you need to start reframing?

Questions for Reflection

- In which area of life do you believe it would be the hardest for you to create closeness? What makes it so?
- In which would it be the easiest? What makes it so?
- What's one idea about "how relationships should be" that's holding you back? How might you reframe it by viewing it through the lens of closeness?

An Exercise to Challenge Yourself

Choose one of the mental hurdles reframed — one you'd like to believe in more. Write it down on a Post-it note and place it somewhere you will see every day, such as the bathroom mirror. Keep it up until you no longer need to process it when you see it. When you no longer need to think about it, it's become a part of your thinking.

Chapter Summary

- We collectively have some outdated ideas about what certain relationships in certain contexts should look like. These ideas get in the way of closeness and become much more helpful when they are reframed.

The Three Big Mental Hurdles at Work

1. "Closeness sounds too intimate for work." Reframed: "Closeness doesn't have to cross any boundaries, and it can actually make teams function better!"
2. "It's inappropriate to talk about feelings at work." Reframed: "Feelings are inextricable from people and from working environments. They are unavoidable, so let's work with them!"
3. "At work, sometimes people really *are* the problem." Reframed: "Let's give people the benefit of the doubt and assume the problem is separate from the person's character until proven otherwise."

The Three Big Mental Hurdles in Families

1. "I grew up with you, I already know you. What more is there to learn?" Reframed: "I can't assume I know your answer before I even ask you a question!"
2. "I can't be honest with my family — telling them too much just makes them worried, disappointed, or critical." Reframed: "Every family member is unique, and there may be one or two I can get close to."

3. "My family is not a family of equals. It's more like a hier-archy." Reframed: "I might not be able to get super close to my family members, but a little closer is better than super distant."

The Three Big Mental Hurdles in Friendships

1. "I just want to have fun with my friends; I don't want to have heavy conversations all the time!" Reframed: "A handful of meaningful conversations will make the fun times even more fun!"
2. "It's kind of weird to take friendships so seriously, espe-cially new ones." Reframed: "I'm not being too serious; I'm being intentional about my relationships."
3. "I've had the same friends forever. I don't feel like I can act any differently than I've always acted with them." Re-framed: "If I have friends but am feeling lonely, there's probably something lacking in my friendships. What might that thing be?"

The Three Big Mental Hurdles in Romance

1. "I don't want my husband or wife to create closeness with anyone but me." Reframed: "Closeness and love are different. Our love can be exclusive, while closeness is shared with many."
2. "The relationship-as-separate-entity thing sounds really unromantic." Reframed: "The relationship-as-separate-entity is actually super romantic because it's an active, conscious creation!"
3. "I don't get how you can be married and have different values." Reframed: "It's being unaware of each other's values that really causes problems."

Chapter 15

Getting Closer to Yourself

A s we approach the end of our exploration of loneliness and of its antidote, closeness, it's time to address the most important relationship you'll ever have in your life: the one you have with yourself.

When someone wants to improve her relationship with herself, she typically says she wants to learn to "love herself." As you might guess, I would challenge the notion that "loving yourself" is a reliable framework for gaining more understanding of and affinity for yourself. If generating love *between* people can't be controlled, I'd suggest that attempting to generate love within yourself is also an uncertain effort.

I believe that when people say they want to love themselves more, what they are really looking for is closeness with themselves. They want insight into their own truest selves, and they want to feel as if their truest selves have worth. This is closeness, and it absolutely can help solidify your relationship with yourself.

Fortunately, not only is becoming closer to yourself possible, but many of the principles you've already learned apply to this new endeavor. As with other relationships, feeling closer to yourself requires the active efforts of knowing and caring — but this time it's knowing and caring about *you*. This is easier than you might think, and the process can be truly joyous.

Beyond fulfilling the desire to love yourself, there are two practical reasons why it's worth it to become closer to yourself. The first is that having at least a bit of closeness with yourself is essential to attaining closeness with someone else. Take knowing, for example. If you know little to nothing about your own inner world — your needs, values, preferences, desires, rhythms — it's going to be extremely challenging for anyone else to know you either. It may not even be possible for someone else to access your inner world if you have not accessed it yourself.

The second reason I recommend taking this step is that you can do it regardless of how many people are in your life at the moment. It's unlikely that you have *no one* who's willing to be even a little closer, but if you do — don't despair! Becoming closer to yourself does not require anyone but you and makes closeness available to you anytime, anywhere. Even better, you may find that becoming closer to yourself alleviates your loneliness in and of itself. You may find that closeness with yourself is what you needed all along.

Knowing yourself well and caring about yourself deeply will make you feel more secure, more authentically yourself, and more resilient to loneliness in the future. You will also gain:

- More access to your inner world
- More understanding of your needs and values
- Greater ability to recognize and express your feelings
- More awareness of how to care for yourself
- More readiness for a significant relationship in your life
- Greater ability to let yourself be known and cared about

Let's look at the top ten ways to create closeness in the most important relationship of all — the one you have with yourself.

Start with Attractions

In the same way you're naturally attracted to certain qualities in other people, you're likely also attracted to certain qualities in yourself. You may be proud of the fact that you always work hard. You may like your ability to see humor in all situations — to see the lighter side of life. You may feel confident that you have a warm heart or a capable mind. These are the qualities you are drawn to in yourself.

Just as with other people, these are the things you'd like to know more about and should pursue. When you like something about yourself, that is your intuition sensing that there's something good in that characteristic, that habit. It doesn't matter how surface level the attraction is, even if it's as simple as liking that you always text people back right away. Follow that quality, and it'll lead you to even more information about what you like about yourself.

Recognizing these attractions is also extremely useful for creating closeness with others because these are often the same qualities others will be attracted to in you. Understanding them will make you more aware of the types of people you're attracting. This is excellent information for you to have as you pursue closeness with others.

 Exercise

List ten things you like about yourself. They can be deep or surface level or a mix of both.

Touch the Surface of Your Inner World

To begin getting to know yourself well, notice, identify and become consciously aware of your wants. Wants are the first entry point for deeper understanding of yourself, just as they are with other people.

I recommend not sitting down and deliberately asking yourself, "What do my wants mean?" This will create anticipation and anxiety around the process of identifying your wants, which will likely lead to internal resistance. Instead, simply be in the moment, and when you find yourself desperately wanting to buy the pair of shoes you saw in a store window, pause for a second. Ask yourself, "What do these shoes get me?" This is a spur-of-the-moment opportunity to uncover the source of a want.

Don't worry if a need or value doesn't instantly spring to mind. You may get an equally "wantlike" response to your question, such as "they look so cool" or "I want to wear those to work on Monday." The goal is to continue investigating — don't let these opportunities escape you. If your initial answer is that the shoes look cool, what does "cool" mean? What would having cool shoes get you? Where does cool lead you?

This, of course, doesn't mean you shouldn't buy the shoes! If they make you feel good, go for it. But making yourself more consciously aware of your actions, drives, and impulses gives you greater understanding of yourself — not to mention the fact that you'll be much better equipped to answer these types of questions when you partner poses them.

 Exercise

Carry a small note pad with you (or use your phone) to write down your wants when they arise. Later, look back over the list and notice wants that may be connected to something deeper.

Gain Deeper Understanding

It's now time to really dig into the underlying sources of your wants — your needs and values. As you know, needs are nearly universal, and unmet needs usually express themselves as complaints. So start noticing: What am I complaining about? What do I feel angry about? Where am I starting to function poorly? Where do I want to point the finger of blame? These are your areas of unmet needs.

Values are a bit more challenging to uncover. Identifying and learning to honor your values is a lifelong project, so allow for fluidity, and let it evolve. Start by paying attention to the times when you feel down, withdrawn, or are asking yourself, "What's the point?" These low points are likely hiding a disregarded value. As unpleasant as these feelings are, they're replete with valuable information for you. They are fingers pointing at what you care about.

If you can identify even a single solid value, you can start honoring it. Ask yourself: How would you show this value you care? Where is it suffering in the world? Where could it use support, encouragement, or nurturing?

You could even think of this work as "getting close" to your values. If you value the environment, for example, get to know and care about the environment. Learn about what it needs. Feel the feeling of caring about it. Getting close to your values ultimately brings you closer to yourself.

 Exercise

Imagine one of your values as an actual person. What would you do to get close to it?

Allow Yourself to Wonder

One of the more challenging ways to apply closeness principles to yourself is by asking yourself inviting questions. It can be quite difficult to hold an inviting mind-set when you already have a lifetime of preconceived notions about what your answers should be. It's also a real challenge to ask yourself an unexpected question — how can it be unexpected if you thought of it?

That being said, question asking is still useful when it comes to getting closer to yourself. Questions are still the best way to drill down into specifics — to get to the details. They simply have to be framed in a different way when you pose them to yourself.

When asking questions of yourself, present them as *curiosities*. Throughout the day, notice what you're doing, saying, or thinking and become curious about it. I wonder what that's about. I wonder what doing this is getting me. I wonder what's making me feel this way. I wonder how this could be different.

As you can see, these are not questions in the literal sense, but more of a pondering about your deeper intentions and motivations. Wondering about yourself in this way removes the pressure to instantly "know the answer" that often causes us to tense up. Just as when you're posing questions to other people, interrogating shuts down the conversation...and "why" doesn't work. A well-crafted question, when you're posing it to yourself, should feel spacious and accommodating. You're just wondering, after all.

 Exercise

As Eric Maisel, writer and creativity coach, suggests: "Go to sleep with a 'sleep thinking prompt' that orients [your] brain toward solutions." Try these three "sleep thinking prompts" over three different nights and write down what you learn!

1. I wonder what I need more of.
2. I wonder what I need to be done with.
3. I wonder what's next.

Write Your Own Narrative

In the same way that listening to another person's narrative gives you insight into how he sees the world — how his "lens" was formed — writing down your own narrative gives you this same insight into yourself. The act of committing your life story to paper will make you aware of the struggles you've overcome, the lessons you've learned, and the vision that propels you forward.

Writing about your past can be a challenge, especially if it's a less-than-happy story. If it feels hard, start where you are. Do you feel scared about writing it down? What's the fear about? Is there a certain story you just can't get out of your mind? Are you struggling to remember the past? What are you not saying? Notice how you're feeling, what you're remembering, and what you're not remembering.

When writing about your future, make it a real story. Nothing is written in stone, so allow yourself to dream. What are some of the best things that could happen to you? What does a perfect day look like five years from now? Notice how these questions make you feel: thrilled, hopeful, terrified, depressed? This is all priceless information about your inner world.

Keep in mind that you can always edit your story. This is your tale to craft — feel free to let go of the bits that no longer feel necessary. What, by contrast, are the really vital parts to remember? Who are the major characters? What are the overarching themes? It's within your control to tell your story in a way that serves you.

 Exercise

To make the project manageable, start with one life event you want to commit to paper (or to a Word document). What was the best day of your life so far? What was the hardest decision you ever had to make?

Feel Your Feelings

Asking you to fully embrace your emotions may be a tall order. But if you want to get closer to yourself, that's indeed what you will need to do. There's really no way around it — you won't know yourself well or be able to care about yourself if you can't feel your feelings.

That being said, you don't need to open the floodgates of emotion all at once. Start by trying to feel one thing a day...and I mean *physically feel it*. Even if it's just a sensation — a pleasant breeze that brings a momentary smile to your face. If you don't feel much, notice any feeling in your body when it arises and hold the belief that the more you feel, the more you *will* feel.

From there, you'll want to start identifying exactly what you're feeling. Put a name to it, such as sadness or disgust, and try expressing it in words. Learning to verbalize feelings is essential in establishing an emotional bond with another person. Your future partner won't ever really know what you're feeling if you can't tell her.

Managing how you express your feelings is a very complex task, but for our purposes here, keep two things in mind: Be still with your soft emotions and challenge your hard emotions. Try not to shut down your soft emotions in fear of them or allow your hard emotions to spiral out of control. Eventually, you'll become skilled at integrating these emotions back into your picture of yourself, leading to much more self-knowledge and self-care.

 Exercise

The next time you feel a hard emotion — anger, frustration, jealousy — commit to challenging it. What is this feeling *really* about? Is it doing me any good to feel this way?

Separate Yourself from Problems

There's likely no better thing you can do to connect with yourself than to start humanizing yourself. You, just like your partner, are fully human. You are precious and valuable but will inevitably make mistakes. As you know, holding this stance allows you to separate yourself from your problems. If you accidentally forgot to get your friend a birthday present, you are human, and you need to solve the problem of not getting your friend a birthday present. If you're late to a job interview, you are human, and you have to put in safeguards to ensure you're not late the next time. You are human, and there are problems. Both things can be true at once.

Holding this mind-set allows you to go hard on the problem and soft on yourself. It allows you to forgive yourself, even when you've created a problem in your own life. Take responsibility for your part in the problem's creation, follow through on resolving it, and then forgive yourself wholeheartedly. Guilt and shame play a huge role in people's resistance to getting close to themselves. They also perpetuate destructive behaviors. Separating yourself from problems may not wipe all guilt and shame away, but it certainly helps.

Last, go ahead and embrace your vulnerabilities. The things you feel insecure about sharing are precious and valuable, just like the rest of you. In fact, many vulnerabilities can be reframed as strengths. Maybe "being a worrier" is also "thinking through all the options." Maybe "being obsessive" is "the ability to focus on one thing." Take time to rethink your vulnerabilities. These are your unique gifts — part of what makes you you!

 Exercise

What are you holding back when you interact with people? What are you worried other people will find out about you? The answers to these questions likely contain one of your vulnerabilities. Reframe it in your mind as a strength, and then share it with someone.

Show Yourself You Care

When showing yourself you care, grand gestures are great, but it's really the small moments that matter. In this way, showing yourself you care is very much like showing someone else you care. You can't give yourself a big spa day once a year and expect it to make up for a lifetime of putting yourself last. To show yourself you care, your moment-to-moment actions should always include the message "I care about myself."

So how do you do this? You start by being responsive to your own needs, by being engaged with your internal self. If you need a moment to yourself, take a moment to yourself. If you need time to process something, take time to process. If you need to stand up for yourself, stand up for yourself.

And above all, give yourself the gifts that you would expect any good partner to give you: appreciation, respect, encouragement, comfort. There's no reason why these can't become an integral part of your relationship with yourself. Making them so builds the inner trust that you can and will take care of yourself in the future.

 Exercise

Spend ten minutes journaling about what it would look like to be more engaged with yourself. Consider:

- What has your body been asking for that you've been ignoring?
- What has your mind been asking for that you've been ignoring?
- What has your spirit been asking for that you've been ignoring?

Create a Culture of Closeness with Yourself

In the same way you're always creating a culture with another person (whether or not you're aware of it), you're always creating a culture with yourself. When you go out of your way to stop at your favorite coffee place every morning, that's a ritual. When you get an image of your favorite flower tattooed on yourself, that's a symbol.

This is already happening, so why not make your inner culture intentionally awesome? Fill your home with symbols and objects that mean something to you and that remind you what you mean to yourself. Go on adventures all by yourself and make memories that will last a lifetime. Look at your values and see where you can start putting them into action — how they can be transformed into purpose. There's no reason to wait to do these activities until you have a partner. Start making meaning and purpose now!

Doing these things with intention makes your relationship with yourself resilient. You'll have daily reminders that you matter to yourself. You'll see your inner world reflected back to you...all around!

 Exercise

Establish some rituals and routines just for you. Make it a habit to take a day trip alone once a month. Go wherever you want, and use the time to reconnect with yourself.

Manage Your Technology Mind-Set

Last, there is the challenge we all face: managing technology's influence on how we interact. I recommend that you become mindful of the ways technology is working well in your life and the ways you're using it as a crutch to ease the discomfort of feeling isolated. Where this line is drawn will be different for each person, but it's great to start thinking about where your line might be.

Beyond that, I always recommend the following:

- Make your own opportunities to find people to get close to, since technology has made our environment less inclined to provide these opportunities organically.
- Take attractions off-line and into the real world as soon as you can. Use technology in service of meeting in real life, not as a tool to avoid doing so.
- When communicating, pick the medium that contains the most layers of nonverbal communication. Remember that the medium through which you communicate (particularly when investigating someone's inner world) can alter the tone of the conversation entirely.
- Last, be conscious of the discovery mind-set. The things you want to know about another person won't surface on their own; you'll have to search for them. Embrace the search. It's half the fun.

 Exercise

When you're feeling lonely, step away from the computer and the phone, at least for a few hours. At this moment, these are distractions. Remember: you're not alone...because you have yourself. When you're physically alone and feeling lonely, spend time with someone who truly knows and cares about you — yourself!

To conclude, it's not only possible to create closeness with yourself; it's a process that will enhance your life in many ways. You will be more prepared to create closeness with someone else. Every exercise you practice with yourself will ultimately make you a better partner. Further, improving the relationship you have with yourself will in and of itself make you less lonely. In truth, you're never alone if you have yourself.

Questions for Reflection

- How well would you say you know your deeper intentions and motivations? If another person asked you questions about the sources of your wants, could you answer them easily?
- In what ways do you show yourself that you care? Are these ways working well for you? How could they be improved?
- Which one of the above exercises is most difficult for you? What about it intimidates or scares you?

 An Exercise to Challenge Yourself

Complete all ten exercises above!

Chapter Summary

- Becoming closer to yourself is possible, and many of the principles you've already learned apply. As with other relationships, feeling closer to yourself requires the active efforts of knowing and caring — but this time it's knowing and caring about *you*.

- There are two primary reasons it's worth your time to become closer to yourself. First, it's essential in attaining closeness with someone else. You will be easier to know and care about if you already know and care about yourself. Second, you can become closer to yourself even when you don't have a willing partner. It makes closeness available to you anytime, anywhere.

    Ten great ways to get closer to yourself are:

    1. Notice what you are attracted to in yourself.
    2. Become aware of your wants.
    3. Investigate the deeper sources of your wants.
    4. Question yourself by allowing yourself to ponder your deeper motivations and intentions.
    5. Write down your life story.
    6. Allow yourself to really feel at least one feeling a day.
    7. Separate yourself from your problems.
    8. Show yourself you care by being responsive to your own needs.
    9. Create a culture of closeness with yourself.
    10. Manage your technology mind-set.

- Use these tools to establish a life in which you are never alone — because you have yourself!

Conclusion

Us vs. Loneliness

From the first time I remember being around people, I remember being lonely. This isn't to say my childhood was in any way bad or traumatic — it wasn't. I grew up in a wonderful family and retain no memories of anyone rejecting, ostracizing, or bullying me. In fact, I remember everyone in my young social circle seeming nice and likable. I think they found me nice and likable as well. They were perfectly good people, and it seemed, so was I. We were just *strangers*.

With the exception of my immediate family, I consistently struggled to get close to others until I was in my midtwenties. I always had friends. At the very least, I always had people with whom I could eat lunch in peace. But inside, I found people *difficult*. I felt like I was doing all the work of trying to connect and would leave most interactions feeling exhausted. Did everyone feel like this? Clearly not. I roiled in jealousy of those who effortlessly gained energy from the company of others.

I decided, around age sixteen, that I must be a purebred introvert and retreated to the privacy of my room. Unless I was 99 percent sure I would have a good time, I politely declined social gatherings. I enjoyed my time alone. I could think, read, and listen to music. I genuinely liked being alone... until I didn't. There was always a moment, usually an hour or two after the party would have started, when I'd feel searing loneliness. I'd beat myself up. Why did I shun these opportunities? People weren't rejecting me, I was rejecting them!

With every declined invitation came the guilt, shame, and confusion. If I was so lonely, why did I isolate myself? The answer was clear to me: I didn't really enjoy being around people. But if I didn't enjoy being around people, why did I get lonely?

As most people in this circumstance do, I blamed myself. I must be responsible for this oscillation between chosen aloneness and loneliness. Everyone else seems to know how to have fun, I thought. What's wrong with me that I don't? Am I too sensitive, too easily overstimulated? Am I too judgmental, too quick to tire of perfectly nice people? I must not be open enough; I must not be trying hard enough.

This struggle shadowed my whole young life. But as I grew older, and my social contexts started to change, I cobbled together a nice life for myself. I found career success as a performance marketer at gaming start-ups. I noticed that the more serious environment of work was more conducive to my feeling comfortable around people than the party environment of college had been. I liked the people at work. When I went home, I felt excited to see them the next day.

In particular, I started to like a guy named Kamo, who, through somewhat random circumstances, became my manager at a gaming start-up in 2011. He was very assertive — teetering on the edge of pushy — truthfully, not someone I would typically like. But as a manager, he channeled his pushiness into an insistence that everyone on his team bond. Specifically, he pushed all of us to recognize one another as people — as more than just the owner of this project or that. He pushed us to get to know each other.

To accomplish this, he arranged for each of us to speak in pairs, in private, every few days. We did not talk about work; we talked about our lives. We talked about how we were doing — in the larger sense. We showed interest in each other. We offered each other help. It didn't matter how many items were on our to-do lists or how many fires needed to be put out; these one-on-ones took precedence. By Kamo's logic, fires went out faster and more efficiently if we all felt connected.

Of course, neither he nor I knew at the time that what we were actually doing was knowing and caring. That idea came much later. At the time I only knew that, after a few months of this deliberate, structured team bonding, Kamo knew me better than anyone else in my life — by far. He also seemed to genuinely care about my well-being. How strange for this to happen at work, of all places — with my boss!

I couldn't help but wonder: What had really happened here? Our coworkers thought we were falling in love (a valid argument, since Kamo and I did indeed get married a few years later). But at that time we both vehemently denied that it was love, because it wasn't. It was something everyone on the team felt. It was something that — blasphemous as it sounds — was kinda better than love. It was *closeness*.

And here I was…surprisingly less lonely because of it. I say surprisingly not only because it happened at work but also because it happened while I remained exactly who I'd always been. I was fundamentally the same as that sixteen-year-old — introverted, sensitive, and all. What had changed? It was not *me* as a person. It was not Kamo as a person — he was as assertive and pushy as ever. What changed, I understood later, was *what we were doing*.

In relationships — romantic, family, and certainly business — you're supposed to have good communication, right? But what does one actually *do* to have good communication? You're supposed to have trust, right? But what does one *do* to have trust? You're supposed to have a bond, right? But what does one *do* to have a bond?

This, I realized, was the problem behind my perpetual loneliness: we all know what we're supposed to *have* in relationships — good communication, trust, fun, respect, compassion, and on and on — but we don't know what we're supposed to *do*. The vast majority of us, including all the strangers from my childhood, are lovely people with good intentions. We just have no idea what to actually do to get close.

Kamo and I changed what we had in our relationship not by changing who we were but by changing *what we did*. You are now fully equipped to do this too. The ideas, tools, and techniques you've learned in this book will guide you through what to do to get what you want from relationships with others.

But before we conclude, there's one last thing I'd like to ask you to start doing. I want you to start separating yourself from the problem of loneliness. You are a precious, valuable human — just like I am — and loneliness is a problem that exists out there, in the world. Loneliness is not a personality trait. It is not a character flaw. I believed that my loneliness was caused by my own shortcomings, until one day I found myself no longer lonely and yet the same person I'd always been.

Our new kind of loneliness is a problem completely separate from you or me or any individual in particular. It's caused by our society's collective ignorance about what to do to have the kinds of relationships we want. It's caused by a status quo for interacting with one another that many people find unfulfilling. It's caused by modern inventions that blur the line between what's being alone and what's being together. It's caused by environmental factors that didn't work for me and haven't been working for you, either.

The beauty is that, as with any external problem, you can

eliminate loneliness from your life. I needed another person to help me see that the loneliness wasn't inside me — that it could be eliminated without my having to change my fundamental nature. I hope I've been that person for you. From here on out, you and I are on the same team working against the problem of loneliness. Let's work together to resolve it once and for all. The truth is, you are already on your way.

Appendix

Reminders and Takeaways

The lists below summarize the key points of this book and offer some ways to stop being lonely now. Use them as reminders and inspiration whenever needed.

The Top Ten Ideas in *Stop Being Lonely*

1. We are experiencing a new kind of loneliness — a loneliness of the heart and mind. It no longer works to just be around people; you must actually *feel close* to them.
2. Only a new solution can address this new kind of loneliness. This solution is closeness, direct access to another person's inner world. Closeness eliminates the internal distance between people and the sadness caused by it.
3. Beyond being the antidote to loneliness, closeness is also the foundation of all happy and satisfying relationships.
4. You create closeness through two specific actions: knowing and caring. Knowing means seeing another person's life from his perspective. Caring means feeling and showing that his well-being matters to you.
5. Our environment, specifically our personal technology, is reducing our natural opportunities to get close to one

another. Our social environment is full of obstacles that lonely people have to actively overcome.

6. Forget about love as a reliable solution to loneliness. If love finds you, that's great...but don't wait for love to come before you stop being lonely. Love is a mystery; closeness is not.

7. All relationships lie on a single spectrum — from distant to close.

8. No relationships are inherently closer than others. Any relationship can be close through the specific efforts of knowing and caring, and any relationship can be distant if these efforts are lacking.

9. Closeness can be created with anyone who also wants to be closer to you, regardless of the context in which you know each other. Friends, family, romantic partners, and business partners are all viable closeness partners.

10. You can create closeness in the relationship you have with yourself. Getting closer to yourself gives you deeper understanding of yourself and helps you recognize that you are valuable.

Ten Key Points to Remember

1. You are in control of your loneliness.

2. You can learn closeness and model it for others.

3. Direct access to another person's inner world is possible and profound.

4. Relationships are not static states; they are active creations.

5. You are not to blame for your loneliness. You are not flawed or unlovable.

6. Create your own opportunities to get close to others.

7. Culture is always being formed, so shape yours intentionally.
8. Give your closeness partner what you'd like to receive in return.
9. Parents, children, bosses, employees: we are all fundamentally human.
10. Do just a little bit — just one thing — and you'll feel less lonely today.

Ten Skills to Practice

1. Challenge your assumptions about what wants mean.
2. Ask a question in fewer words than you think possible.
3. Sit with another person's strong emotion.
4. Give moments, and ask for moments.
5. Share something about yourself that feels risky.
6. Model a behavior you'd like your partner to adopt.
7. Demonstrate interest in your partner, even when it's difficult.
8. Calm your physiology when you're feeling agitated.
9. Notice when you're speaking from a stance of superiority.
10. Forget what you're planning to say and just listen — deeply listen.

Ten Simple Ways to Start Now

1. Approach *one potential partner* and strike up a conversation.
2. Ask *one question* you would have felt too awkward to ask before.
3. Take *one hour* to write down the first draft of your life story.
4. Take responsibility for *one thing* you could have done better in a relationship.

5. Pause for *one minute* and get yourself straight before launching into a fight.
6. Tell *one person* you're ready to forgive her.
7. Let go of *one relationship* that is distant and not worth the effort to make closer.
8. Spend *one day* entirely away from personal technology.
9. Make *one disclosure* to your partner that's highly private.
10. Give your partner *one moment* when she needs it...and trust that she will give you a moment in return.

Notes

Introduction

2 *In 2006 the* American Sociological Review *reported:* Miller McPherson, Lynn Smith-Lovin, Matthew E. Brashears, "Social Isolation in America: Changes in Core Discussion Networks over Two Decades," *American Sociological Review* 71, no. 3 (June 2006), asr.sagepub.com /content/71/3/353.short.

Chapter 1. What Is Closeness?

15 *True intimacy with others is one of the highest values:* Karen J. Prager and Linda J. Roberts, eds., "Deep Intimate Connection: Self and Intimacy in Couple Relationships," in *Handbook of Closeness and Intimacy*, ed. Deborah Mashek and Arthur Aron (Malwah, NJ: Lawrence Erlbaum, 2004), 43.

16 *The study was launched in 1938:* Brett and Kate McKay, "Love Is All You Need: Insights from the Longest Longitudinal Study on Men Ever Conducted," *Art of Manliness*, September 2, 2014, www.artofmanliness .com/2014/09/02/love-is-all-you-need-insights-from-the-longest -longitudinal-study-on-men-ever-conducted.

17 *We saw consistency in the sense:* Emily Caldwell, "Loneliness, Like Chronic Stress, Taxes the Immune System," *Ohio State University Research News*, January 19, 2013, researchnews.osu.edu/archive/lonely.htm.

17 *[Our] findings indicate that the influence of social relationships:* Julianne Holt-Lunstad, Timothy B. Smith, J. Bradley Layton, "Social Relationships and Mortality Risk: A Meta-Analytic Review," *PLOS Medicine*

(July 27, 2010), journals.plos.org/plosmedicine/article?id=10.1371
/journal.pmed.1000316.

Chapter 2. An Environment of Obstacles

24 *It's been proven that everyone lies*: Katie McDonough, "Study: When It
Comes to Online Dating, Everyone's a Little Bit of a Catfish," *Salon*,
February 27, 2013, www.salon.com/2013/02/27/study_when_it
_comes_to_online_dating_everyones_a_little_bit_of_a_catfish.

24 *The company that created a similar app*: "The World's Top 10 Most Inno-
vative Companies in Social Media," *Fast Company*, February 13, 2014,
www.fastcompany.com/3026321/most-innovative-companies-2014
/the-worlds-top-10-most-innovative-companies-in-social-media.

24 *Share anonymously with friends*: Secret's CrunchBase profile, accessed
May 15, 2015, www.crunchbase.com/organization/secret.

25 *These 24-hour friendships expire*: Nicholas Miller, "Meet Sobrr, a New
Social Network that Erases Everything after 24 Hours," *VentureBeat*,
July 10, 2014, venturebeat.com/2014/07/10/meet-sobrr-a-new-social
-network-that-erases-everything-after-24-hours.

26 *By some accounts, nonexplicit communication*: Blake Eastman, "How Much
of Communication Is Really Nonverbal?" *Nonverbal Group*, August 2011,
www.nonverbalgroup.com/2011/08/how-much-of-communication
-is-really-nonverbal.

27 *Google defines the word* efficient: Google search engine results for "efficient definition," accessed May 22, 2015, www.google.com/?gws
_rd=ssl#q=efficient+definition.

28 *A comprehensive study published by AARP*: Knowledge Networks and
Insight Policy Research, "Loneliness among Older Adults: A National
Survey of Adults 45+," *AARP The Magazine*, September 2010,
http://assets.aarp.org/rgcenter/general/loneliness_2010.pdf.

28 *Nearly 60% of those aged 18 to 34*: Clare Murphy, "Young More Lonely
Than the Old, UK Survey Suggests," *BBC News*, May 25, 2010, news
.bbc.co.uk/2/hi/health/8701763.stm.

Chapter 3. Dispelling Old Myths

37 *The earliest evidence of family life*: Mary Jo Maynes and Ann Waltner, *The
Family: A World History*, Kindle ed. (Oxford: Oxford University Press,
2012), 1.

38 *Different societies have different definitions*: Maynes and Waltner, *Family*, x.

39 *Families are small groups of people*: Maynes and Waltner, *Family*, x.

39 *As the preeminent "care marketplace"*: "Company Overview," Care.com, accessed May 15, 2015, www.care.com/company-overview.

43 *Jeff Bezos, founder of Amazon.com*: Janet Choi, "The Science behind Why Small Teams Work More Productively: Jeff Bezos' 2 Pizza Rule," *Buffer Social*, July 29, 2013, blog.bufferapp.com/small-teams-why-startups-often-win-against-google-and-facebook-the-science-behind-why-smaller-teams-get-more-done.

43 *Jennifer Mueller coined the term* relational loss: Choi, "Science Behind."

44 *And they couldn't tell their team leader*: Choi, "Science Behind."

44 *A survey published by Gallup showed*: Walter Chen, "The Most Engaged Employees Work at Companies of 10 People and Fewer," *iDoneThis Blog*, June 14, 2013, blog.idonethis.com/the-most-engaged-employees-work-at-companies-of-10.

Chapter 4. Learning to Pick Partners

47 The Bachelor *is absolutely brilliant*: "The Bachelor," *Wikipedia*, last modified July 15, 2015, en.wikipedia.org/wiki/The_Bachelor_(U.S._TV_series).

52 *But evidence shows that we start constructing*: California Institute of Technology, "Snap Judgments during Speed Dating," *ScienceDaily*, November 12, 2012, www.sciencedaily.com/releases/2012/11/121112171323.htm.

53 *Crossing the tipping point should be particularly harmful*: Artemio Ramirez, Erin M. (Bryant) Sumner, Christina Fleuriet, Megan Cole, "When Online Dating Partners Meet Offline: The Effect of Modality Switching on Relational Communication between Online Daters," *Journal of Computer-Mediated Communication* 20, no. 1 (January 2015): 99–114.

54 *Although factual and emotional self-disclosures*: Jean-Philippe Laurenceau, Luis M. Rivera, Amy R. Schaffer, Paula R. Pietromonaco, "Intimacy as an Interpersonal Process: Current Status and Future Directions," in *Handbook of Closeness and Intimacy*, ed. Deborah Mashek and Arthur Aron (Malwah, NJ: Lawrence Erlbaum, 2004), 63.

58 *For the interaction to be experienced as intimate*: Laurenceau et al., 62.

61 *They categorize the two most dangerous personality types*: Jane E. Brody, "Battered Women Face Pit Bulls and Cobras," *New York Times*, March 17, 1998, www.nytimes.com/1998/03/17/science/battered-women-face-pit-bulls-and-cobras.html.

Chapter 5. Gaining Access to Another Person's World

72   *The wedding — which had reportedly cost around $10 million*: Anna North, "Kim Kardashian's Divorce, by the (Incredibly Ridiculous) Numbers," *Jezebel*, October 31, 2011, jezebel.com/5854891/kim-kardashians -divorce-by-the-numbers.

75   *AdoreMe subjects all of its images to testing*: Rebecca Greenfield, "This Lingerie Company A/B Tests the World's Hottest Women to See Who Makes You Click Buy," *Fast Company*, November 21, 2014, www.fast company.com/3038740/most-creative-people/this-lingerie-company -a-b-tests-the-worlds-hottest-women-to-see-who-mak.

75   *Over time the evolution of the internet*: John Rampton, "The Past, Present, and Future of Content Discovery," *Forbes*, September 12, 2014, www.forbes.com/sites/johnrampton/2014/09/12/the-past-present -and-future-of-content-discovery.

76   *An article published on Inc.com*: John Boitnott, "A.I. Is Helping the Inter-net Know What You Want before You Want It," *Inc.*, October 7, 2014, www.inc.com/john-boitnott/ai-is-helping-the-internet-know-what -you-want-before-you-want-it.html.

Chapter 6. Drawing Deeper Understanding

82   *The most enduring framework for understanding needs*: Saul McLeod, "Maslow's Hierarchy of Needs," *Simple Psychology*, 2007; updated 2014, www.simplypsychology.org/maslow.html.

92   *As social psychologist and relationship expert*: Susan E. Cross and Jonathan S. Gore, "The Relational Self-Construal and Closeness," in *Handbook of Closeness and Intimacy*, ed. Deborah Mashek and Arthur Aron (Malwah, NJ: Lawrence Erlbaum, 2004), 235.

Chapter 7. Asking Inviting Questions

96   *To get a sense of the importance of questions*: Mandy Len Catron, "To Fall in Love with Anyone, Do This," *New York Times*, January 9, 2015, www.nytimes.com/2015/01/11/fashion/modern-love-to-fall-in-love -with-anyone-do-this.html?

96   *The article, written by Mandy Len Catron*: Arthur Aron, Edward Melinat, Elaine N. Aron, Robert Darrin Vallone, Renee J. Bator, "The Experi-mental Generation of Interpersonal Closeness: A Procedure and Some

Preliminary Findings," *Personal Social Psychology Bulletin* 23, no. 4 (April 1997): 363–77, psp.sagepub.com/content/23/4/363.full .pdf+html.

106 *I first read about the classic negotiation scenario*: Roger Fisher, William L. Ury, Bruce Patton, *Getting to Yes: Negotiating Agreement without Giving In*, Kindle ed. (New York: Penguin, 1981; repr., 2011), loc. 1271.

Chapter 8. Listening to Another Person's Narrative

115 *Rather, it is the remembering self*: Jennifer Senior, *All Joy and No Fun: The Paradox of Modern Parenthood*, Kindle ed. (New York: Harper-Collins, 2014), loc. 4060.

Chapter 9. Feeling Another Person's Feelings

134 *The hijacking occurs in an instant*: Daniel Goleman, *Emotional Intelligence* (New York: Bantam/Dell, 2006), 14.

136 *New research suggests there may be as few as four*: Julie Beck, "New Research Says There Are Only Four Emotions," *The Atlantic*, February 4, 2014, www.theatlantic.com/health/archive/2014/02/new-research -says-there-are-only-four-emotions/283560.

140 *He then asked each partner to watch the video*: Robert W. Levenson and John M. Gottman, "Physiological and Affective Predictors of Change in Relationship Satisfaction," *Journal of Personality and Social Psychology* 49, no. 1 (July 1985): 85–94, Ist-socrates.berkeley.edu/~ucbpl/docs /28-Physiological%20and%20affective%20predictors85.pdf.

144 *But over the five-day period they improved drastically*: Sarah Thomas, "Thanks to Technology, Young People Are Losing the Ability to Read Emotions," *International Business Times Australian Edition*, August 29, 2014, au.ibtimes.com/thanks-technology-young-people-are-losing -ability-read-emotions-1352279.

Chapter 10. Uniting as a Team

149 *As Roger Fisher describes*: Roger Fisher, William L. Ury, Bruce Patton, *Getting to Yes: Negotiating Agreement without Giving In*, Kindle ed. (New York: Penguin, 1981; repr., 2011), loc. 672.

150 *For example, it is now well known that happily married couples*: Jean-Philippe Laurenceau, Luis M. Rivera, Amy R. Schaffer, Paula R. Pietromonaco, "Intimacy as an Interpersonal Process: Current Status

and Future Directions," in *Handbook of Closeness and Intimacy*, ed. Deborah Mashek and Arthur Aron (Malwah, NJ: Lawrence Erlbaum, 2004), 71.

156 *As researcher and vulnerability expert Brené Brown put it*: Brené Brown, "The Power of Vulnerability," TED talk transcript, December 2010, www.ted.com/talks/brene_brown_on_vulnerability/transcript? language=en.

Chapter 11. Making a Relationship

160 *Collaborative production is simple*: Clay Shirky, *Here Comes Everybody: The Power of Organizing without Organizations* (New York: Penguin, 2009), 50.

161 *When this threshold is crossed*: Debra J. Mashek and Michelle D. Sherman, "Desiring Less Closeness with Intimate Others," in *Handbook of Closeness and Intimacy*, ed. Deborah Mashek and Arthur Aron (Malwah, NJ: Lawrence Erlbaum, 2004), 348.

166 *An article about the company ran on* Forbes*'s website:* Karsten Strauss, "Is This the Fastest-Growing Game Company Ever?" *Forbes*, April 17, 2013, www.forbes.com/sites/karstenstrauss/2013/04/17/is-this-the-fastest -growing-game-company-ever.

166 *As its name implies, Supercell is organized*: Neil Rimer, "Why We Invested in Supercell," Index Ventures blog, April 17, 2013, www.indexventures .com/news-room/blog/why-we-invested-in-supercell.

170 *In the early 1990s, a team of neuroscientists*: Ben Thomas, "What's So Special about Mirror Neurons?" *Scientific American* guest blog, November 6, 2012, blogs.scientificamerican.com/guest-blog/whats-so-special -about-mirror-neurons.

172 *We propose that desiring less closeness with someone*: Mashek and Sherman, "Desiring Less," 344.

Chapter 12. Showing Another Person You Care

175 *In its own words, Invisible Boyfriend*: Invisible Boyfriend's website, accessed May 22, 2015, invisibleboyfriend.com.

175 *One of the core premises of Invisible Boyfriend*: Caitlin Dewey, "I Paid $25 for an Invisible Boyfriend, and I Think I Might Be in Love," *Washington Post*, January 22, 2015, www.washingtonpost.com/news/the-intersect /wp/2015/01/22/i-paid-25-for-an-invisible-boyfriend-and-i-think-i -might-be-in-love.

181 *The results indicated that both "visible" support*: Natalya C. Maisel and Shelly L. Gable, "The Paradox of Received Social Support," *Psychological Science* 20, no. 8 (August 2009): 928.

186 *We feel sad and think we should not feel sad*: Dan Wile, *After the Fight: Using Your Disagreements to Build Stronger Relationships* (New York: Guilford Press, 1993), 9.

Chapter 13. Creating a Culture of Closeness

195 *This is why people who win the lottery*: "Connection & Happiness," *This Emotional Life*, accessed May 22, 2015, www.pbs.org/thisemotionallife /topic/connecting/connection-happiness.

195 *Close relationships, however, may be an exception*: "Connection & Happiness."

196 Merriam-Webster's Dictionary *defines the word culture*: *Merriam Webster's Dictionary*, accessed May 22, 2015, www.merriam-webster.com /dictionary/culture.

196 *Rather than membership in monolithic groups*: Glenn Adams, Stephanie L. Anderson, Joseph K. Adonu, "The Cultural Grounding of Closeness and Intimacy," in *Handbook of Closeness and Intimacy*, ed. Deborah Mashek and Arthur Aron (Malwah, NJ: Lawrence Erlbaum, 2004), 322.

199 *Home objects "cue relationship qualities to the couple themselves"*: Ximena B. Arriaga, Wind Goodfriend, Andrew Lohmann, "Beyond the Individual: Concomitants of Closeness in the Social and Physical Environment," in *Handbook*, 296.

202 *Every experience is being mediated*: Nick Bilton, "Disruptions: More Connected, Yet More Alone," *New York Times* blog, September 1, 2013, bits.blogs.nytimes.com/2013/09/01/disruptions-more-connected-yet -more-alone/?_r=1.

Chapter 14. Overcoming Obstacles at Work, at Home, and in Love

212 *The study gave participants electronic badges*: Alex "Sandy" Pentland, "The New Science of Building Great Teams," *Harvard Business Review*, April 2012, hbr.org/2012/04/the-new-science-of-building-great -teams.

212 *Together those two factors explained*: Pentland, "New Science."

Chapter 15. Getting Closer to Yourself

232 *Go to sleep with a 'sleep thinking prompt'*: Eric Maisel, "30 Days to Better
Mental Health," *Psychology Today*, January 1, 2015, www.psychologytoday
.com/blog/rethinking-psychology/201501/30-days-better-mental-health.

Index

About the Author

Kira Asatryan, a certified relationship coach, lives in San Francisco with her husband, a Silicon Valley entrepreneur. She is a graduate of the University of California, Berkeley, and provides individual life coaching, relationship systems coaching, conflict mediation, and couples' coaching. Before becoming a relationship coach, she was director of performance marketing for prominent Silicon Valley technology start-ups and cofounded an online marketing consultancy. Kira maintains a private coaching practice in the San Francisco Bay Area.